History in English Words

Owen Barfield

History in English Words

Introduction by W.H. Auden

Lindisfarne Press

First published by Faber & Faber, London in 1953
Revised edition published by Eerdmans,
Grand Rapids, Mich., in 1967

Republished in 1985, 1988 by the Lindisfarne Press, Box 778, Great
Barrington, MA 01230.

Printed in the United States of America
10 9 8 7 6 5 4

ISBN 0-940262-11-8

CONTENTS

FOREWORD

I have drawn from the well of language many a thought which I do not have and which I could not put into words.

C. G. Lichtenberg

Many who write about 'linguistics' go astray because they overlook the fundamental fact that we use words for two quite different purposes; as a code of communication whereby, as individual members of the human race, we can request and supply information necessary to life, and as Speech in the true sense, the medium in which, as unique persons who think in the first and second person singular, we gratuitously disclose ourselves to each other and share our experiences. Though no human utterance is either a pure code statement or a pure personal act, the difference is obvious if we compare a phrase-book for tourists travelling abroad with a poem. The former is concerned with needs common to all human beings; hence, for the phrases given, there exist more or less exact equivalents in all languages. No poem, on the other hand, can be even approximately translated into any other language. A poet, one might say, is someone who tries to give an experience its Proper Name, and it is a characteristic of Proper Names that they cannot be translated, only transliterated. Furthermore, precisely because writing poetry is a gratuitous act, in it, as Valéry observed, "everything which *must* be said, is almost impossible to say well."

Whereas most code statements are verifiable or disprovable, most personal utterances are neither; they can only be believed, doubted or denied. When we speak as persons, capable of good and evil, the important question is not 'Is what we say the case or not?', but 'Are we speaking the truth, or deceiving ourselves, or deliberately lying?'

Many animals possess a code for communicating vital information about food, sex, the presence of enemies, etc., and in social animals like the bee this code may be extremely complex. It is even possible that, in the case of animals, geese, for example, which are capable of forming personal bonds between individuals, their sound-and-gesture code may have an element of personal expression but, even if this be so, it is secondary, whereas, in the case of human language, personal speech is its primary function, to which its use as a code is subordinate.

If this were not so, then, like all other species, we should only have one language, used and understood by all human beings, with at most slight regional dialect differences, like the song of the chaffinch, and this language would undergo no historical change, but remain the same from generation to generation. But from the beginning, not only have men spoken many different languages, all subject to historical change, but also no two persons with the same mother-tongue speak it in exactly the same way. Understanding what another human being says to us is always a matter of translation. In this book, Mr Barfield is trying to help us to translate correctly, instead of making, as we all too often do, the most elementary errors.

Foreword

True understanding is unattainable without both love and detachment, and we can only learn to view anything with detachment by comparing it with other things which are both like and unlike it. We cannot understand the present without a knowledge of the past, our native land without having spent some time in a foreign country, our mother-tongue without a working knowledge of at least two other languages. Without such knowledge, our love of ourselves at the present moment, of our country, of our language, remains an ignorant idolatry, exemplified by the Frenchman who said: "The great advantage of the French language is that in it the words occur in the order in which one thinks them."

In weaning us from this idolatry, the historical approach employed by Mr Barfield seems to me much more likely to be effective than the approach of the linguistic analysts. The latter seem to believe that, by a process of 'demythologising' and disinfecting, it should be possible to create a language in which, as in algebra, meanings would be unequivocal and misunderstanding impossible. But human language is mythological and metaphorical by nature. As Thoreau said: "All perception of truth is a perception of an analogy; we reason from our hands to our heads." Mr Barfield gives many fascinating illustrations of this process. The English words *delirious* and *prevaricate*, for example, are derived from the Latin verbs, *delirare* and *praevaricari*, which originally meant, he tells us, 'to go out of the furrow' and 'to plough in crooked lines'. A secular and, therefore, fool-proof language is an unphilosophical daydream. We can only cope with the dangers of language if we recognize that language is by nature magical and therefore highly dangerous. It will always be possible to use language, as a demagogue uses it, as Black Magic which neither, like a communication code, supplies people with information they need to know, nor, like Speech, asks for a personal and therefore unpredictable response, but seeks to extort from others mindless tautological echoes of itself.

"We must not forget," Mr Barfield reminds us, "that nine-tenths of the words comprising the vocabulary of a civilised nation are never used by more than at most one tenth of the population; while of the remaining tithe, nine-tenths of those who use them are commonly aware of about one-tenth of their meanings."

Until quite recently, this did not matter very much. Before the spread of semi-literacy and the development of the mass media, the language used by the nine-tenths was the language they had learned at first-hand from their parents and their next-door neighbors. Their vocabulary might be limited, they might be aware of many of its possible meanings, but with it they were able to say what they meant to say and to understand what was said to them. Their ignorance of historical changes in the meanings of words was not a serious handicap because they could not or had no desire to read the literature of the past. The age of innocence, however, has come to an end and can never return. To-day, when all school children and college students are expected to read some English Literature, the consequence of such ignorance is that a nineteen-year-old, confronted with the lines,

> *The agèd bloodhound rose and shook his hide,*
> *But his sagacious eye an inmate owns.*

can interpret them as follows: "The poor dog was blind.

10

Some lunatic had punched his eye out and kept it."

To-day we must modify Mr Barfield's warning and say that nine-tenths of the population use twice as many words as they understand. It is no longer a matter of their knowing some of the possible meanings of the words they use; they attach meanings to them which are simply false. Thus one can hear a person, when he is feeling sick, say *I am nauseous;* a reviewer of a spy-thriller can describe it as *enervating;* a famous television star can call a firm of investment brokers, for which he is making a plug, *integrity-ridden.* So befuddled, how can the man-in-the-street be expected to resist the black magic of the propagandists, commercial and political? Formerly, philology could remain a study for specialists: to-day, *History in English Words*, and other books like it, must be made required reading in all schools.

I have deliberately refrained from saying much about the contents of Mr Barfield's book. After reading it, one first impulse is to tell others about the many facts in it which have surprised and delighted one. I never knew before, for instance, that the first recorded use of the word *self-respect* in a favorable sense—hitherto it had always been a pejorative, akin to *selfishness*—occurs in Wordsworth's poem *The Excursion.* One's second impulse is to cite further examples of significant meaning-changes. I am fascinated, for example, by euphemisms and would very much like to know exactly when it was first thought tactful to call the poor *under-privileged* and the old *senior citizens.* But, on reflection, one realises that asking such questions is a form of showing off, and that to quote extensively from a book of this kind is as bad as telling readers in advance the solution to a murder mystery.

It is a privilege to be allowed to recommend a book which is not only a joy to read but also of great moral value as a weapon in the unending battle between civilisation and barbarism. As Dag Hammarskjöld wrote in *Markings:*

> *Respect for the word is the first commandment in the discipline by which a man can be educated to maturity —intellectual, emotional and moral.*
>
> *Respect for the word—to employ it with scrupulous care and an incorruptible heartfelt love of truth—is essential if there is to be any growth in a society or in the human race.*
>
> *To misuse the word is to show contempt for man. It undermines the bridges and poisons the wells. It causes Man to regress down the long path of his evolution.*

— W. H. Auden

PART I

THE ENGLISH NATION

I

PHILOLOGY AND THE ARYANS

ELECTRIC · QUALITY · GARDEN · MEAD · TIMBER

I f somebody showed us a document which he said was
an unpublished letter of Dr. Johnson's, and on reading
it through we came across the word 'telephone', we
should be fairly justified in sending him about his business.
The fact that there was no such thing as a telephone until
many years after Johnson's death would leave no doubt
whatever in our minds that the letter was not written by
him. If we cared to go farther, we could say with equal certainty that the letter was written since the beginning of the
nineteenth century, when the telephone was invented.

Now suppose that there had been nothing about tele-
phones in the letter, but that it had contained an account of
a thunder-storm. If in describing the stillness just before the
storm broke the writer had said that 'the atmosphere was
electric', we could still be fairly positive that he was not
Dr. Johnson. But this time it would not be because the
thing of which the letter spoke had no existence in Johnson's
day. No doubt the heavens during a storm a hundred and
fifty years ago were as highly charged with electricity as
they are today; but if we look up the word *electric* in the

Oxford Dictionary, we find that in Johnson's time it simply was not used in that way. Thus, in his own dictionary it is defined as:

'A property in some bodies, whereby when rubbed so as to grow warm, they draw little bits of paper, or such-like substances, to them.'

The world was only just beginning to connect this mysterious property of amber with the thunder and lightning, and however still and heavy the air might have been, it would have been impossible for the lexicographer to describe it by that word. Or again, supposing the letter had said nothing about a storm, but that it had described a conversation between Garrick and Goldsmith which was carried on 'at high tension', we should still have little hesitation in pronouncing it to be a forgery. The phrase 'high tension', used of the relation between human beings, is a metaphor taken from the condition of the space between two electrically charged bodies. At present many people who use such a phrase are still half-aware of its full meaning, but many years hence everybody may be using it to describe their quarrels and their nerves without dreaming that it conceals an electrical metaphor—just as we ourselves speak of a man's 'disposition' without at all knowing that the reference is to astrology.[1] Nevertheless by consulting an historical dictionary it will still be possible to 'date' any passage of literature in which the phrase occurs. We shall still know for certain that the passage could not have been written in a time before certain phenomena of static electricity had become common knowledge.

[1] See p. 142.

Thus, the scientists who discovered the forces of electricity actually made it possible for the human beings who came after them to have a slightly different idea, a slightly fuller consciousness of their relationship with one another. They made it possible for them to speak of the 'high tension' between them. So that the discovery of electricity, besides introducing several new words (e.g. *electricity* itself) into our everyday vocabulary, has altered or added to the meaning of many older words, such as *battery, broadcast, button, conductor, current, force, magnet, potential, tension, terminal, wire*, and many others.

But apart from the way in which it is used, there is a little mine of history buried in the word *electric* itself. If we look it up in a dictionary we find that it is derived from a Greek word 'ēlektron', which meant 'amber'. And in this etymology alone anyone who was completely ignorant of our civilization could perceive three facts—that at one time English scholars were acquainted with the language spoken by the ancient Greeks, that the Greeks did not know of electricity (for if they had there would have been nothing to prevent our borrowing their word for it), and that the idea of electricity has been connected in men's minds with amber. Lastly, if we were completely ignorant of the quality of amber itself, the fact that 'ēlektron' is connected with 'ēlektōr', which means 'gleaming' or 'the beaming sun', might give us a faint hint of its nature. These are some of the many ways in which words may be made to disgorge the past that is bottled up inside them, as coal and wine, when we kindle or drink them, yield up their bottled sunshine.

Now the deduction of information from the presence or absence of certain words is a common practice which has been known to critics and historians of literature, under some such name as 'internal evidence', for many years. It is from such evidence, for instance, that we deduce Shakespeare's ignorance of the details of Roman civilization. But until a few years ago—within the memory of men still living—very little use had been made of language itself, that is to say, of the historical forms and meanings of words as interpreters both of the past and of the workings of men's minds. It has only just begun to dawn on us that in our own language alone, not to speak of its many companions, the past history of humanity is spread out in an imperishable map, just as the history of the mineral earth lies embedded in the layers of its outer crust. But there is this difference between the record of the rocks and the secrets which are hidden in language: whereas the former can only give us a knowledge of outward, dead things— such as forgotten seas and the bodily shapes of prehistoric animals and primitive men—language has preserved for us the inner, living history of man's soul. It reveals the evolution of consciousness.

In the common words we use every day the souls of past races, the thoughts and feelings of individual men stand around us, not dead, but frozen into their attitudes like the courtiers in the garden of the Sleeping Beauty. The more common a word is and the simpler its meaning, the bolder very likely is the original thought which it contains and the more intense the intellectual or poetic effort which went to its making. Thus, the word *quality* is used by most educated people every day of their lives, yet in order that we should have this simple word Plato had to make the tremendous effort (it is one of the most exhausting which man is called on to exert) of turning a vague feeling into a clear thought. He invented the new word 'poiotēs', 'what-ness', as we might say, or 'of-what-kind-ness', and Cicero translated it by the Latin 'qualitas', from 'qualis'. Language becomes a different thing for us altogether if we can make ourselves realize, can even make ourselves feel how every time the word *quality* is used, say upon a label in a shop window, that creative effort made by Plato comes into play again. Nor is the acquisition of such a feeling a waste of time; for once we have made it our own, it circulates like blood through the whole of the literature and life about us. It is the kiss which brings the sleeping courtiers to life.

But in order to excavate the information which is buried in a word we must have the means to ascertain its history. Until quite recently (about a hundred years ago) philology, as an exact science, was still in its infancy, and words were derived by ingenious guesswork from all kinds of impossible sources. All languages were referred to a Hebrew origin, since Hebrew was the language of the Bible. This was taken for granted. Since then, however, two new developments have revolutionized the whole study, made it accurate, and enormously extended its scope. During the eighteenth century Sanskrit, the ancient speech of the Hindoos, began for the first time to attract the attention of European scholars. In 1767 a French Jesuit named Coeurdoux pointed out certain resemblances between the European and Sanskrit languages. In 1786 Sir William Jones described that language as being

'of wonderful structure; more perfect than the Greek, more copious than the Latin, and more exquisitely refined than either, yet bearing to both of them a stronger affinity, both in the roots of verbs and in the forms of grammar, than could have been produced by accident—so strong that no philologer could examine all three without believing them to have sprung from some common source which, perhaps, no longer exists.'

At the time it was no more than a brilliant conjecture, but with it the comparative philology of the Aryan languages may be said to have begun.

Secondly, with the advent of phonology certain apparent laws were discovered governing the sounds made by the human throat and the way in which these sounds change with the passing of time and react upon each other when they are knit together in a spoken word. Henceforward it was possible to say for certain that, for example, the English word *wit* (from the old verb 'witan', to know) was not *derived* from the Latin 'videre', but cognate, or related, with it. Many words derived from 'videre', such as *advice, envy, review*, seem at first sight much farther off from the stem 'vid-' than *wit*, but it was now possible for scholars to say definitely that a Latin stem 'vid' adopted into English could not possibly have changed into *wit*. They could be equally certain that, if the Romans had *borrowed* the Greek word 'idein' (to see) into their language, it could never have changed its form to '*vid*ere', so that, innumerable as are the words which Rome borrowed from Greece, 'videre' is not one of them. Thus, it was clear that such groups of three words as *idein, videre*, and *wit*, or *astēr, stella*, and *star*, were not father, son, and grandson (as is the case, for instance, with *poeinē, poena*, and *penal*), but three brothers or cousins all descended from a common ancestor with a stem something like 'weid' belonging to some other language. This, put very briefly and with many omissions, was the contribution made by phonology to the science of comparative philology.

Perhaps it is not altogether insignificant that the study of that seemingly dull subject—phonology—should be associated in our minds with one of the most charming collections of fairy-tales in Europe. It is thanks to the labours of Jacob Grimm during the first half of the last century that we are now able to reconstruct the remote pasts of words, not, it is true, with absolute certainty, but with a degree of it which makes a chapter such as the present one worth writing. And while Grimm was burrowing into the rich, loamy soil of German speech and German folk-lore, another German scholar, Franz Bopp, was laying the foundations, with the help of this knowledge and of the results of the study of Sanskrit, of a genuinely scientific comparative philology. Nor was it long before less scholarly but more imaginative minds, such as Max Müller's, were interpreting the meaning of their researches to a wider public.

We can imagine the suppressed excitement of the philologists of that time as they began to discover in that remote Eastern language, the sacred language of the Vedic hymns, words such as 'vid' (to see), 'tara' (a star), 'sad' (to sit), 'bhratar' (a brother). For it was not only the evident relation of Sanskrit to the languages of Europe that was exciting. Sanskrit, which had preserved the forms of its words more unchanged than any other Aryan tongue, threw a brilliant light on the close relations existing between those other languages themselves. For instance, although the sisterhood of words such as the Greek 'onoma', Latin 'nomen', and *name*, had long been suspected, yet there had been no way of distinguishing such a sisterhood from purely accidental resemblances like Hebrew 'gol', Greek 'kaleo', and *call*, and the connection between 'brother' and 'frater' was by no means obvious. But when the older Sanskrit form 'bhratar' was brought to light, the gap between these words was at once bridged. It could be seen at a glance how the three of them, *brother*, *bhratar*, and *frater*, had started from the same original form and diverged through the years. Gradually all doubt was blown away, and Sanskrit, the language of a race with whom Europeans had thought, and for the most part still think, that they had almost nothing in common, stood revealed as an obvious relative of Latin, Greek, Modern English, and practically all the other languages of Europe. It seemed, therefore, to follow that our ancestors and those of the Hindoos were at one time living together, that our ancestors and theirs were, in fact, the same.

At first it was thought that Sanskrit itself was the parent-language from which all the others had derived, and that the nations of Europe were descended from a body of Hindoos, some of whom had migrated westwards. We called ourselves 'Aryans' because the people who had once spoken Sanskrit were known as 'Aryas', or worshippers of the God of the Brahmins. But soon the accurate methods of analysis which philology had now acquired made it plain that this could not be so. Therefore a still older language was postulated and called indifferently the Aryan, the Indo-Germanic, or the Indo-European parent-language. If there was a language, there must have been a people who spoke it, and attention was soon focused on the character, civilization, and whereabouts in space and time of the people who spoke the lost Indo-European, or 'Aryan' parent-language.

The fascination of this particular branch of philological research is apparent when we recollect that in this case, in the case of these remote Eastern ancestors—or predecessors —of ours, philology is almost the only window through which we can look out on them. In most subsequent periods of history we have many other ways, besides the study of language, of discovering the outward circumstances of men's lives. Historical records, archaeology, ethnology, folk-lore, art, literature, all come to our help in considering, say, the ancient Egyptian civilization; but it is not so with the Aryans. Here ethnology and archaeology tell us practically nothing, anthropology a little, and the rest nothing at all. If we wish to cross the darkness which separates us from this period we must lay down a little plank of words and step delicately over it. And in such romantic circumstances it is hardly surprising that we should find a veritable army of scholars and philosophers, both professional and amateur, jostling each other upon that plank with such vigour that the bridge and its burden have often seemed in danger of vanishing quietly together into the abyss.

The central principle upon which philologists have worked is this, that if a word occurs today in a fair sprinkling of the Aryan languages, then that word existed in the Aryan parent-language, and therefore the thing of which it is the label existed in some form or other in the primitive Aryan civilization. Conversely, if an object or an idea is found to have a different name in most of the Aryan languages, it was sometimes assumed that that object was not known to the Aryans before their dispersion. But this negative deduction soon came to be regarded as unsafe, and there are indeed many reasons why the whole method is limited and uncertain. For instance, even in one language it is constantly happening that, when a new thing or a new idea comes into the consciousness of the community, it is described, not by a new word, but by the name of the pre-existing object which most closely resembles it. This is inevitable. We have to proceed from the known to the unknown in language as in life; but language lags behind life and words change more slowly than things or ideas. When railways first came in, their rolling-stock consisted of a string of vehicles resembling the old horse coach so exactly that it was said later that 'the ghost of a horse stalked in front of the engine'. Although this is no longer the case, we still call these vehicles *carriages* or *coaches*, and look like continuing to do so. To take an even more patent example, when a modern Englishman or American uses the very old Celtic word *car*, we all know what he means: yet it would be an error to deduce from this that the principle of internal combustion was known in pre-Christian times in Wales, Ireland, Cornwall, Brittany, and probably Rome (Latin 'carrus', a cognate word). Moreover, we can see at once that the fraction of error is very much greater when we are dealing, not with the development of a word in one language, but with its history as it descended from one language to another; for example, from the hypothetical parent-tongue into the languages with which we are familiar today. Indeed, this kind of reasoning, if no other evidence were available, would lead us to conclude that the Greeks were acquainted with electricity.

Fortunately, however, it is not the object of this little book to put forward theories and discuss the extent to which they can be proved or disproved by words. And though it has been interesting to observe that in some cases —and notably when we are endeavouring to reconstruct the life and thought of our Aryan ancestors—our knowledge, such as it is, is derived very largely from the evidence of words, yet in these pages, even when that particular period is being dealt with, the words chosen for description will by no means necessarily be those which provide the most conclusive evidence for what is said. A great deal has been done in quite recent years by way of collating the results of comparative philology with those of anthropology, ethnology, comparative mythology, etc., and reconstructing from the combined data something of the past history of our own and other races or cultures. We are concerned here, not with the way in which those results were arrived at, but with the results themselves. The reconstruction itself has been and is being done by scholars; here the endeavour is rather to make use of their labours; not to think about the past, as it were, but to look at it. Consequently the words chosen are not the most useful ones, but those which are the best telescopes; for while the nineteenth century spent itself prodigally in multitudinous endeavours to know what the past was, it is now possible for us, by penetrating language with the knowledge thus accumulated, to feel how the past is.

Who are the Aryans? Where did they come from? Looking back down the corridor of time from the particular perspective to which we have attained in the twentieth century, far away in the past—it may be in the Stone Age—

we seem to be able to perceive a remarkable phenomenon. At some particular spot in the vast plains stretching from Eastern Europe to Central Asia it was as though a fresh spring bubbled up into the pool of humanity. Whether it represented the advent of a new 'race-type', what a race-type exactly is, and how it begins are questions which we must leave to others to settle. That spring was the Aryan culture.

Throughout much of Europe and Asia there were already in existence different civilizations in different stages of development; such were the Egyptian, the Chaldean, and farther west the great Minoan civilization, which in its Bronze Age was to ray out an influence from Crete all over the Aegean world. It may be that there was something static[1] in the very nature of these pre-Aryan cultures, or it may be that they were ageing and passing in the natural course of events; what is certain is that there was something dynamic, some organic, out-pushing quality in the waters of this Aryan spring. For these waters spread. They have been spreading over the world ever since that time, now quickly, now slowly, down into India and Persia, north to the Baltic, west over all Europe and the New World, until in the persons of the three Aryan explorers, Peary, Amundsen, and Scott, their waves have licked the poles. It appears to have been the tendency of the Aryan settler, whether he came as a conquering invader or as a peaceful immigrant, to obliterate more than he absorbed of the aboriginal culture on which he imposed himself. In this the Celts and

---

[1] The linear writing of Cretan inscriptions has been pointed to by one writer as a sign of this passivity. Philologists have also pointed out the important position occupied by the verb in Aryan speech.

Teutons who ages ago overran most of Europe appear to have resembled the English-speaking settlers who long afterwards almost annihilated the North American Indian with his gods and traditions. It is true that we English owe to this latter pre-Aryan race the ability to express just that shade of contempt which is conveyed by the word *skunk*, also the charming blend of whimsicality and reprobation crystallized in *mugwump*. But such survivals really only emphasize the extent to which, as the Aryan waters spread, the pre-Aryan past has been covered over. The past does indeed live in the language we speak and in those with which we are familiar, but it is the past of the Aryans. If we dig down far enough into the English language, we reach an old civilization flourishing somewhere round the banks of the Dnieper; of what was going on in these islands at that time we hear scarcely the faintest reverberation.

There is little doubt that the ancient inhabitants of Western Europe as a whole differed from their Aryan successors in two important customs. They buried their dead, whereas the Aryans invariably used cremation; and they were organized in systems of matriarchies. Aryan culture is patriarchal to its foundations. We may patronize our less fortunate neighbours, but we do not 'matronize' them. Yet faint memories of such strange ways seem to have lingered on among the Aryans in the widespread legend of a race of Amazons who once dwelt in the lost continent of Atlantis, the western land, and in the rumour of mighty female warriors in pre-Celtic[1] Gaul, while the name of the River Marne (Matrona) has been said to be another relic of the

[1] Gaul was inhabited by Celts at least as early as the third century B.C. The *Galli*, against whom Caesar fought, were Celtic tribes.

existence in pre-Aryan Europe of a race of men who deified their trees and streams, and hoped, when they died, to be gathered to their mothers.

With this brief glance at our forgotten forerunners, we may turn our gaze upon that region near the banks of the Dnieper whence our own ancestors first began to expand into the world. And we get a glimpse of the kind of settlements in which these pastoral people must have lived in the fact that the English word *garden* has grown from the same stem as the termination *-grad* in *Petrograd*, where it means 'town', while on the other hand the Dutch for *garden* is 'tuin'. We see their villages, family settlements springing up in an enclosure round the home of a patriarch. Households are large and cumbersome, the sons, as they grow up, bring home wives from different villages, and all live together under the roof and absolute dominion of the mother and father-in-law. Both sexes wear *zones* or loincloths, and probably in addition one simple garment of fur or of some woven material, which does not altogether hide their tattooed bodies, adorned with armlets and necklaces of animals' teeth, or it may be of shells or amber beads. It is the business of the women in these communities, not only to remain faithful to their husbands on pain of the most appalling penalties, not only to bring up the children, to keep house, and to *weave* and spin, but also to till the fields and look after the *bees, geese, oxen, sows*, and such other animals as may have been domesticated. A hard enough life, but they have their consolations as they grow older and become respected as dames. Moreover, they have a religious cult of their own. In some cases their imaginations are rich in myth, and they are looked up to as knowing the secrets of Nature and possibly of the future itself. It is the men's business to make war, hold councils, and hunt—possibly with horses[1] and *hounds*, both of which animals are at any rate known to them. The family lives on a kind of unleavened bread, *milk*, cheese,[2] cooked meats, vegetables, and some fruits.

There is much brutality. Widows may be expected to join their husbands in the grave, and old men are sometimes killed off to make room; nevertheless, life is not without its friendlier aspect. There is little doubt, for instance, that our Aryan ancestors knew how to get drunk. The liquor, made principally of honey, with which they sent themselves to bed, appears to have been fraught with such sweet associations that no branch of the Aryan family, however far they went upon their travels, could forget it. The Angles and Saxons brought this *mead* into our country, and the word occurs in Dutch, Icelandic, Danish, Swedish, German, Irish, Lithuanian, Russian, Greek ('methu'), Sanskrit, Zend, and modern Persian. As it threads its way through this babel of tongues, ringing the changes on the meanings of 'honey', 'drunkenness', and 'enjoyment', the little monosyllable seems to give us a peculiarly intimate peep into the interior of an Aryan home. Yet the connection of the word *bed* with the Latin stem 'fod-' (fodio), 'to dig', should prevent us from forming an unduly voluptuous image of the final stages of this prehistoric pastime. If we call up before us a roof and walls of wood or wattles, bounding a dark interior crowded with human beings and possibly some cattle, lit only by a draughty hole in the roof

[1] Greek 'hippos'; Lithuanian 'asva', etc.
[2] Greek 'turos', from which was formed 'bouturon' (butter).

—an arrangement which the Teutons were evidently trying to express when they afterwards dubbed it a 'wind's eye' or *window*—we have a picture which will serve. It is a picture of our ancestors just before they began to spread out over the world, and the time is before 2000 B.C.

But the question of the houses in which they lived takes us farther back still. At some time, probably before they became acquainted with agricultural modes of livelihood, the Aryans were living a nomadic existence. *Axle, nave, wheel, yoke,* and a common word for 'waggon' have convinced people that they once moved from place to place in a kind of primitive caravan, running probably on solid wheels (for there is no common word for 'spoke'). Now the English word *cove,* which in its Icelandic form means 'hut' and in its Greek form ('gupē') a subterranean dwelling such as that which was inhabited by the Cyclops, takes us back to a still older form of residence. Again, *wand* in English means a 'slender rod', but in German and Dutch it means a 'wall', while the weightier and more solid word *timber* is connected with the Greek root 'dem-' (demein), 'to build', Latin 'domus', 'a house'. In these words we can perhaps see the most ancient house rising as time goes on out of a natural cave in the ground to the dignity of a sort of dug-out with wattled sides and roof—eventually to the estate of a firm, wooden hut. And so, behind the picture of our ancestors as they lived together on the spot from which they finally began to spread, we can discern another less certain picture of the very beginnings; of a race, a family perhaps, or some voluntary collection of men not tied by blood, who were together in the Stone Age somewhere in Central Asia. They increase in numbers and power, and, trekking westwards, live—for how many years or centuries we cannot tell—as a race of pastoral nomads, until somewhere in the region of the Dnieper they pass from the wandering nomad existence to some more settled life such as that which has been described.

In addition to the somewhat prosaic words from which we have attempted to derive information, it is pleasant to us to think of these ancestors of ours already uttering to one another in that remote past great and simple words like *fire*, *night*, *star*, *thunder*, and *wind*, which our children still learn to use as they grow up. And we must think also how during all this time the new thing, the force, the spirit which the Aryans were to bring into the world, must have been simmering within them. Strengthening their physique through the generations by stricter notions of matrimony, working by exogamy upon their blood, and through that perhaps upon some quality of brightness and sharpness in their thought, the Aryans became—Aryans.[1] And then they began to move. And the result was the *Bhagavad Gita*, the Parthenon frieze, the Roman Empire, and the Holy Roman Empire—it was Buddha, Michelangelo, the plays of Shakespeare, Bach, Goethe—it was Aristotle and Bacon, and the vast modern industrial civilizations of Europe, Britain and America reaching out to the Antipodes.

[1] Terms such as 'nation', 'race', 'ancestors', 'descendants' are used in these chapters loosely, and without intending political or ethnological implications. The people referred to as 'Aryans' are the people who spoke the Aryan language. They are clearly our cultural 'ancestors', and that is really the only concern of this book, which was written several years before the word 'Aryan' had been adopted as a racial shibboleth by the Nazi Party in Germany.

II

THE SETTLEMENT OF EUROPE

BEECH · BARD · ATTIC · TRAGEDY · AUTHORITY
DELIRIOUS · WINE · CHURCH

It would be a great mistake to picture the Aryans setting out in some vast, organized expedition such as that of the Israelites under Moses. The study of comparative grammar suggests rather that they spread outwards from their centre in a series of little rills, each one, as it flowed, either pushing the rill in front of it a stage farther on, or flowing through it and passing beyond. During the first thousand years of this process we have very little idea of the extent to which the individual groups of these ever-widening circles—the different 'races' as they were perhaps now beginning to be—were in communication with one another. After a time, however, we can discern them pretty sharply divided into two streams, a north-western and a south-eastern stream. It was the main stream which flowed north-west, and it carried along with it the ancestors of the powerful races which were afterwards to be called Greeks, Italians, Slavs, Teutons, and Celts. The settlement of the Celts in Britain and the subsequent arrival first of the Teutonic Angles and Saxons and then of the Normans, the movement of the Celts westward to Wales and Ireland, and the final streaming of their Teutonic successors right through them and across the Atlantic—all these are excellent examples of the way in which the separate rills of the north-western stream have continued ever since the first central commotion to crawl and mingle and overlap like the waves of an incoming tide.

Meanwhile the south-eastern stream flowed past the Himalayas down into India and westward to Persia, where their descendants became the Brahmanic Hindoos and the Zoroastrian Persians of a later date.

That all connection was lost at a very early date between these two main streams is suggested by another interesting little group of words. These are common to all the members of the north-western group, but quite unknown to the south-eastern, and perhaps the most interesting is *mere*, the Old English for 'sea', which is still used poetically of inland waters, and in the word *mermaid*, while its Latin form 'mare' is equally familiar to most educated Englishmen. From the distribution of this word among the Aryan nations, together with similar equations such as *fish* and *piscis*, we can deduce that these two groups of travellers had already separated before either of them reached the sea-board.

There is evidence, too, that this north-western group, comprising as it did the ancestors of the Greeks and Romans, as well as of the Celts, Teutons, and Slavs, had reached, before it dispersed, a new country of forests, such as must have covered most of Northern and Western Europe at that time. At any rate we find words for trees—such as *beech, elm,* and *hazel*—and for birds—*finch, starling, swallow*, *throstle*—common to most of the languages spoken by their descendants, yet absent from Persian and Sanskrit. It was at this time, and amid these surroundings, that agriculture seems to have appeared among the north-western Aryans. The old Aryan word from which we have *acre* lost its former meaning of 'any enclosed piece of land' and acquired the new and special significance of *tilled* land, as in the Latin 'ager', etc. *Corn*, *furrow*, *bean*, *meal*, *ear* of corn, and the verb to *mow* also date back to this period of our history.

And then the north-western stream again sub-divided; and we will follow first of all that branch of it which dropped away southward into the Balkan peninsula and the islands of the Aegean. This time it is not a word, but a poet's imagination which has fixed for us in a passage of considerable beauty the historic moment when this wave first lapped the farther shore, the prophetic shock of contact between Aryan settler and aborigine:

> *Then fly our greetings, fly our speech and smiles!*
> *As some grave Tyrian trader, from the sea,*
> *Descried at sunrise an emerging prow*
> *Lifting the cool-haired creepers stealthily,*
> *The fringes of a southward-facing brow*
>   *Among the Aegean isles;*
> *And saw the merry Grecian coaster come,*
> *Freighted with amber grapes, and Chian wine,*
> *Green bursting figs, and tunnies steep'd in brine;*
> *And knew the intruders on his ancient home,*
>
> *The young light-hearted Masters of the waves. . . .*

These young, light-hearted masters were called Greeks, or Hellenes; they migrated southwards in a series of waves, the first of which contained two tribes known as the Achaians and Danaans. We still make use of some of the experiences undergone by these and other Greek tribes, and of the characteristics which they developed, in order to express more exactly our own inner experiences. Through the channel of words and myths which have come down to us from that time, the great poet who sang to the Achaians and Danaans of the exploits of their ancestors has given us many metaphors and images—special little reservoirs of feeling which we could not have created for ourselves. Most people, for instance, like to be called *Trojans; stentorian, pander,* and *hector* are from the names of characters in his poems, and *nectar* and *ambrosial* from the food and drink consumed by his gods. Speech was a more miraculous and rhythmical thing to the Achaians than it is to us today, and whether or no the Gaelic *bard* is cognate with the Greek 'phrazein', to 'speak', there is no doubt that 'epos', the 'word', had its other meaning of 'poem'. Long afterwards the adjective 'epikos' came to be applied especially to lofty compositions such as those of the great poet himself. Accordingly, in the European war the special correspondent could often find no more vivid expression for his sense of the vastness and grandeur of the catastrophe he was recording than to call up by the word *epic* vague memories of Homer's gods and heroes.

A single timid reference to 'awful signs',[1] together with the absence of any ordinary word for 'writing', suggests that Homer's Achaians did not know how to write, and

[1] σήματα λυγρά.

that his two long poems of twenty-four books each had to be memorized from beginning to end by that class of professional reciters from which our word *rhapsody* is derived. The actual text of the *Iliad* and *Odyssey* gives us a vivid and majestic picture of early, but not the earliest, Aryan culture. Of their author, in so far as there was one particular author, we know very little except that he was probably blind. It was the common thing for the bards who were to be found among all the Aryan races, and survived as 'Minstrels' into the Middle Ages, to be blind; and Homer's own blindness, apart from a reference to it, has been deduced by some from a preponderance in his poems of 'audile' epithets, such as the *clanging* arrow and the *loud-sounding* sea. It may be mentioned that the Slavs once called their bards 'sliepac', a word which also meant 'blind'.

The Dorians settled in Laconia in the southern part of the Peloponnese or, as it is now called, the Motean peninsula. The notorious taciturnity of the inhabitants of Laconia has given us *laconic*, and we are referring to their rigid ideas on infant welfare when we speak of a '*spartan* mother', for Sparta was the capital of Laconia.

Attica, for a time the home of the Ionians (who eventually crossed the Aegean to Asia Minor), has a more complex history; and it was in Attica, in the sixth and fifth centuries b.c., that the Hellenic culture reached its finest flower. We use the word *Attic*[1] to describe a peculiarly finished work of art or an exquisite literary style. No wonder. In the city state of Athens, for the first time among the Aryans, there began to grow up something which an

[1] The modern sense of 'a small room at the top of the house' goes back to the time when *Attic* was also used of architectural refinements, especially that which is achieved by placing a smaller order above a larger one.

educated man of today would be willing to recognize as a civilization. In that clear air of a marvellous political freedom—a social atmosphere which could hardly have condensed from any but Aryan moral ideas—the matured, age-old wisdom of Egypt and the East was absorbed by these youngsters and transformed in a few hundred years into a science, an art, and a philosophy of their own which have never been wholly surpassed. Consequently, the names of many things which we regard as the very hall-marks of a cultured society can be traced back to the Attic dialect of this period. *Academy, school, history, logic, grammar, poetry, rhythm, harmony, melody, music,* are all from Greek works which were in common use in Athens, and the lasting influence of her sublime dramatic tradition is indicated by the great words, *chorus, comedy, drama, theatre,* and *tragedy,* and the lesser *catastrophe, episode, prologue,* and *protagonist,* all of which draw their meanings from the inspiration of the great Athenian dramatists.

Meanwhile another branch of the Aryan family had found its way into Italy, and there, in the eighth century before our era, had founded the city of Rome. It is noticeable that the pitch darkness in which the early doings of all the Aryans are lost often seems to flash into a spark of myth or legend at those moments when they come into contact with other races. It is just such a spark which, in the story of the rape of the Sabine women, perhaps lights up for us one of the early shocks of encounter between Italiot Aryans and the older inhabitants of Italy.

Most people know a little about the subsequent history of these Italiots. The republic which they eventually established at Rome transformed itself into an empire that extended its bounds until they were coterminous with the civilized world—an empire of Europe and part of Asia which retained its real authority oven men's persons until the fifth century A.D., and its authority, as an idea, over their minds and actions down to that day at the beginning of the last century when Bonaparte first styled himself 'Emperor of the French'. There is, in fact, scarcely a word in our language expressing even remotely the notion of 'authority', which does not come to us from the Latin: *authority*, *chief*, *command*, *control*, *dictator*, *dominion*, *empire*, *government*, *master*, *officer*, *rule*, *subordinate*, are some of them; and it is significant that the two Greek words which we use to express the same idea are *despot* and *tyrant*. Both these terms have a definite stigma attaching to them, and are employed very much more often by the foes of authority than by her friends. The Greeks were not the nation to establish a world-empire. They would have combined to bury Caesar, not to praise him; and from another point of view the odious *sybarite* is good proof that they were not the stuff of which colonists are made. The English *lord* and *king*, on the other hand, retain about them a hint of the possibility of affection. It is a mark of affection when sailors drop the Latin *captain* and adopt the Dutch *skipper*, and the substitution by landsmen of Old High German *boss* for Latin *manager* seems to have begun in the same way.[1] And lastly, when we wish to suggest a peculiar blend of dignity and chill self-consciousness, we use

[1] Note, however, that the tendency is now the other way and, with the growth of twentieth-century class-consciousness, *manager* and *managerial* are used where the intention is to express the bare fact of authority without innuendo, while *boss* and *bosses* are pejorative.

the name of the most remarkable of all the Roman emperors.

Rome not only extended her jurisdiction over all Europe; she was responsible for the birth of a new idea in men's minds—the idea that 'authority', as such, based on an abstraction called 'law' and irrespective of real ties of blood or affection, of sympathy or antipathy, of religion or ownership, can exist as a relation between human beings.

But we have hurried on to the Empire and left out the Republic. What were the beginnings and early occupations of this astonishing race, of whose national hero we are reminded when we use the word *brute*? In the previous chapter reference was made to certain words and phrases which are now used for the purposes of everyday life, but which were originally technical metaphors drawn from the phenomena of electricity. If we examine such words as *calamity, delirious, emolument, pecuniary, prevaricate, tribulation*, we shall find that they possess a similar history. Although the Romans of classical times used the Latin words from which they are derived in much the same way as the English words are used now, yet if we trace them a little farther back, we learn that 'delirare' had at one time no other meaning than to 'go out of the furrow', when ploughing; 'praevaricari' was to 'plough in crooked lines'; 'tribulare' to thrash with a 'tribulum', and so forth. In *interval*, on the other hand (from 'intervallum', the space between two palisades), *excel, premium, salary*, and many other words we have examples of metaphors taken from the military life. The English-sounding word, *spoil*, comes to us from a Latin term which once had no other meaning than to 'strip a conquered foe of his arms'. By entering with our imaginations into the biography of such a word, we catch glimpses of civilization in primitive Rome. Agriculture and war, we feel, were the primary businesses of life, and it was to these that the Roman mind instinctively flew when it was casting about for some means of expressing a new abstract idea—of realizing the unknown in terms of the known. Not often could the warlike city afford to beat her swords into ploughshares, but she was constantly melting both implements into ideas.

Wherever we turn in our language, we have only to scratch the surface in order to come upon fresh traces of Rome and of her solid achievements in the world. With Greece, however, it is different. It was not the outer fabric of a future European civilization which the Greeks were building up while their own civilization flourished, but the shadowy, inner world of human consciousness. They were helping to create our 'outlook'. We shall see a little later how the language which is used by the theologians, philosophers, and scientists of Europe was the gradual and painful creation of the thinkers of ancient Greece; and we shall see that, without that language, the thoughts and feelings and impulses which it expresses could have no being. Rome's task was to erect across Europe a rigid and durable framework on which the complicated texture of thought, feeling, and will, woven in the looms of Athens and Alexandria, could be permanently outspread. Yet the performance of this task, concrete as it was, was inseparably connected with an event of tremendous import for that growing, inner world to which we have already referred—the most significant event, as many believe, in the history of mankind.

The first casual contact between Greek coaster and Semitic trader, imaginatively portrayed in the stanza quoted above from Matthew Arnold, was indeed prophetic. It proved afterwards to have been not merely a memorable event, but a sort of fertilization of the whole history of humanity. For to one Semitic tribe the passionate inner world of its thoughts and feelings had remained almost more real than the outward one of matter and energy. The language of the Old Testament is alone enough to tell us that, while the Greek Aryans had been pouring their vigour into the creation of intellectual wisdom and liberty, the Hebrews had been building up within themselves an extraordinary moral and emotional life, as narrow as it was intense. The two streams of evolution, stronger for having been kept apart, were destined to meet and intermingle. In 332 B.C., when Alexander the Great sacked Sidon and Tyre, Greeks and Hebrews began for the first time to live side by side. They did not intermarry, but subtle influences must have passed from one to the other, for in Alexandria, shortly afterwards, contact between the two grew so intimate that by the second century B.C. Greek had become the official language of the Hebrew Scriptures. In the same century a Roman Protectorate was established over Syria, which in course of time became a province of the Roman Empire. In that province was born the individual who is known to history as Jesus of Nazareth.

His teaching, as far as it has come down to us, was Semitic both in its form and in its outlook on the past. Nevertheless, it was His teaching, and the feelings and impulses (though in a somewhat unrecognizable form) which He implanted in the hearts and wills of men, which were spread by the organization of the Roman Empire all over Europe; and it was, above all, that part of the Greek world of thought which had crystallized round His teaching that was carried over into the thought and feeling of modern Europe.

But all this could only happen very slowly; for while Greece and Rome had been rising successively to pinnacles of civilization, the rest of the north-western group of Aryans had remained plunged in darkness. They had passed Italy by, and already, more than a thousand years B.C., begun to spread themselves over the rest of Europe and to develop in the different areas wherein they found a resting-place the distinctive characteristics of Teuton, Slav, and Celt. The Slavs, although they occupied—and still occupy—the whole vast east of Europe, and although they number something like two hundred million souls, have as yet had extraordinarily little influence upon our national life. There are only two adopted Slavonic words which may be described as common in all our language, *trumpet* and *slave*, and both have come to us by devious routes, the first through German and French, the second through Greek and Latin. One of the lesser Slavonic races, the Croatians, developed a kind of neckwear which appealed to the fashionable French, who adopted it and described it as 'croate', 'crovate', or 'cravate', from which we get our *cravat*. Otherwise the words are mostly exotic both in sound and meaning. Thus, those that come to us direct from Russia are *copek, drosky, knout, rouble, samovar, steppe, verst* —all of which, with the possible exception of *steppe*, are still only used when we are speaking of life in Russia itself.[1]

[1] The reader will readily add, for himself, those which have been coming into use since this book was written.

The Settlement of Europe

How different it is when we come to consider the Teutons! When we have abstracted all the Latin words, the French words, the Celtic words, etc., from our vocabulary, the 'English' words which remain are all Teutonic; for we, ourselves, are a branch of the Teutonic race.[1] Accordingly some of our older and most English words contain buried vestiges of the lives which our ancestors once lived in the continental forests. *Fear*, which is thought to be derived from the same word as *fare*, has been taken to suggest the dangers, and *weary*, which is traced to an old verb meaning 'to tramp over wet ground', the fatigues of early travel, while *learn* goes back to a root which meant 'to follow a track'. As the Italiot Aryans, the Romans, created and extended their empire, they came into contact with these barbaric Teutonic tribes, whom they regarded, naturally enough, not as kinsmen, but as strangers. We find some of the results of this contact in such words as *inch, kitchen, mile, mill, pound, street, toll, wall*, and *table*—all of which are Latin words borrowed by our ancestors while they were still living on the Continent together with the ancestors of the Scandinavian, Dutch, German, Austrian, and Swiss nations. By their nature these words suggest civilizing influences, and we find in their company the names of more portable articles, such as *chest, dish, kettle, pillow*, and *wine*, which traders might have brought with them on their beasts of burden. This hypothesis becomes almost a certainty when it is seen that *mule* and *ass* were borrowed from Latin at this

[1] But with a good deal of the Celt in us. There is no exact correspondence between language and blood, the one being a measure of an intellectual, the other of a more directly spiritual heritage. Cf. the influence of the Celts upon the *meanings* of Romance words, pp. 44-45, 93-94, 123, 205.

time; that *-monger* (in *costermonger*, *fishmonger*, . . .) is a corruption of 'mango', the Latin name for a trader; and that
the old English *ceapian*, 'to buy', which we still keep in
chap, *chapman*, *cheap*, . . . goes back to 'caupones', the
Roman name for wine-dealers. A few words like *pepper*
even seem to have come in at this time from the remote
East, by way of Rome, and altogether these old Teutonic
words may indeed give us, as Mr. Pearsall Smith has said,
'a dim picture of Roman traders, travelling with their
mules and asses along the paved roads of the German provinces, their chests and boxes and wine-sacks, and their
profitable bargains with our primitive ancestors'. Finally,
the military words *camp* and *pile* recall the heyday of the
Empire, when Rome would recruit vast armies from her
provincial subjects, and the *-chester*, which terminates the
names of many English towns, is of course Latin *castra*, a
camp. Even *church* (another word common to all the
Teutonic languages) may have been brought home by
German mercenaries on service in the East. The Greek
'Kuriakon', from which it is said to be derived, was in use
in the Eastern provinces, as opposed to the 'ekklesia' (French
'église', Italian 'chiesa' and *ecclesiastical*) adopted by Latin
Christianity, and our pagan forefathers probably picked it
up accidentally while they were pillaging the sacred buildings in which their posterity was to kneel.

The modern nations of Norway, Sweden, Denmark,
Holland, England, Germany, Austria, and Switzerland
cover most of the area over which the Teutonic immigrants originally spread. In a good many cases they found
Celtic predecessors already in possession. These Celts had
been the first Aryans to arrive in Northern Europe, and

they seem, at one time, to have spread over most of the Continent. Later on, in historical times, they were to be found chiefly throughout that wide district—including most of modern France and a great part of Spain and Portugal—which the Romans called 'Gaul', as well as all over Great Britain and Ireland. In Spain and France they mingled their blood extensively with that of the Italiots, the two together becoming the ancestors of the present 'Latin' races or speakers of the 'Romance'[1] languages. But already, long before the decline of the Roman Empire, the Teutons were beginning to drive the Celts westward and away, a process which is clearly marked in these islands by the prevalence of Celtic place-names in the west country. Thus, the percentage of Celtic place-names in Cornwall has been calculated to be about 80; in Devon it is only 32, and in Suffolk 2. The conflict between Celt and Teuton dragged on in Ireland until 1921, and it is doubtful if it is quite finished yet. One contingent of the old Celtic inhabitants of this island, or *Britons*, driven to the tip of Cornwall, decided to leave these shores altogether. They sailed back to the Continent, and there established themselves in the seaboard district which still bears the name of *Brittany*. It is said that a Welsh peasant and a Breton can still, to this day, understand one another's speech well enough for most practical purposes.

The number of proved Celtic words which have found their way into English is extraordinarily small—scarce

[1] Students of the Wordsworthian theory of poetic diction will be interested to learn that the origin of this curious word is believed to be a Late Latin phrase, 'romanice loqui', meaning 'to speak the vulgar Latin of everyday life, as distinguished from book-Latin'.

above a dozen. *Bard*, *bog*, and *glen* are among those which have come to us direct, and *car* had to travel through Latin and French before it reached us, the original having been borrowed by Julius Caesar from the Gauls, who had thus named their war chariots. But for the most part, Celtic words like *banshee, eisteddfod, galore, mavourneen*, . . . have a remote and foreign look, even though we may have used them for many years. When we reflect that the Welsh tongue is still spoken within two hundred miles of London, and that another Celtic language, the Cornish, has only just died out, this seems very difficult to understand.

Such, then, in barest outline, was the distribution of the Aryan races which formed the major part of that vague and loose-knit organization, the later Roman Empire. But it must not be imagined that this picture of Rome's European subjects is anything like complete. Evoking history from words is like looking back at our own past through memory; we see it, as it were, from within. Something has stimulated the memory—a smell, a taste, or a fragment of melody—and an inner light is kindled, but we cannot tell how far that light will throw its beams. Language, like the memory, is not an automatic diary; and it selects incidents for preservation, not so much according to their intrinsic significance as according to the impression they happen to have made upon the national consciousness.

Thus, English words have little to tell us about the great migrations and massacres in Europe during the first ten centuries of the Christian era, for terms of abuse like *vandal* and *hun* draw their emotional force from the imaginations of historians rather than from actual contact with the tribes in question.[1] From a mathematically impartial point of view, therefore, the small amount of space that can be assigned here to events which absorbed such an enormous share of time and energy and swallowed millions of human lives is indeed misleading. There is, however, an interesting little group of words still bearing the imprint of the mighty upheaval which took place around the Mediterranean during the seventh and eighth centuries A.D., when Mohammedan Arabs overran Persia, Syria, Egypt, North Africa, Spain, and the south of France. As might be expected, these words come to us mostly from Arabic, via Spanish and French, for it was in Spain that Islam took her firmest hold on Europe. They include *cotton, gazelle, giraffe, lacquey, masquerade, syrup, tabby* (originally a kind of silk), *tabor, talc, tambourine*, and some very interesting technical terms to which we shall presently return. Naturally the receding tide of invasion has left Arabic place-names dotted about in all the countries mentioned, while Spain herself is crammed with them; but to give examples would be beyond the scope of this little volume, which now finds itself drawn by the laws of its subject-matter to hover more closely about the shores of these islands.

---

[1] *Bigot*, which is found in French as early as the twelfth century, has been connected with *Visigoth*, but this derivation is not regarded as probable.

III

ENGLAND
BEFORE THE REFORMATION

DURBECK · CHESTER · CANDLE · CROSS · LAW
PERSON · CHAIR · OBLIGATION · SIZE

There could hardly be a better example of the un-
easy movement of Aryan migrations than the history of the settlement of the British Isles. We find
them, first of all, as far back as we can look, inhabited by an
unknown population who left their barrows and tumuli
dotted about the country, whose society seems to have
been matriarchally organized, and who, if the name *Pict*
may be taken as any indication, probably had the habit of
painting or tattooing their bodies. At length, several centuries before our era, the first Aryan wave reaches these
shores in the persons of the Celts, who spread over England,
Wales, Scotland, and Ireland, where they have been pointed
out and variously described by historians, as *Britons, Ancient
Britons, Welsh, Gaels, Celts,* . . . They settle down and live
for some centuries the kind of life which we describe as
primitive, till half-way through the first century B.C. they
are disturbed by a little Aryan tongue reaching out from

the wellnigh spent Italian wave. Pagan Rome establishes a brief dominion over a small portion of Britain, drives roads, builds camps and cities, and after some four hundred years is sucked back again to the Continent. Another century, and the Angles and Saxons, borne forward on the crest of the Teutonic wave, overrun the main island, driving the Celts into its extremities, whence they regurgitate, before finally settling down, upon various military and missionary enterprises which have played an important part in our history. But already another ripple of the Teutonic wave is upon us, rocking over the seas in the long boats of the Scandinavian Vikings, and almost before they have left their impress on the eastern quarter of the land, a third—the Normans this time—is breaking on Britain once again at Pevensey. The liquid metaphor is unavoidable, for no other image seems adequate to express what actually happened. To watch through the glasses of history the gradual arrival and settlement of the Aryans in this country is to be reminded irresistibly of the rhythmic wash and backwash, the little accidental interplays of plash and ripple, which accompany the tide as it fills an irregularly shaped pool.

Every one of these motions has left its mark on our language, though the traces of the earliest immigration of all —that of the Celts—are rather scarce. The clearest vestiges of it are to be found in the proper names of our rivers, for a surprising number of these contain one or other of the various Celtic terms for 'water' or 'river', e.g. *avon*, *dwr* (*ter* or *der*), *uisge* (*wye*, *usk*, *is*, *ax*), while the other parts of the name are often composed of words for 'water' taken from another Aryan language, as in *Derwentwater*, *Winder-*

mere, Easeburn, Ashbourne. . . . An ingenious theory has been evolved to account for this. In the case of the *Dur-beck* in Nottinghamshire, and the *Dur-bach* in Germany, it has been supposed that in the first place a body of Celtic immigrants squatted by the side of a stream which, as they were not extensive travellers, they knew simply as the *dwr*— 'The Water'. Their Teutonic successors inquired the name of the stream, and on learning that it was *dwr*, naturally assumed that this was a proper name. They accordingly adopted it, and tacked on one of their own words for 'water'—'bach' or 'beck', just as we may speak of the 'Avon River' or the 'River Ouse'. The phenomenon occurs so persistently both in this country and all over Europe that this explanation can hardly be altogether fanciful.

The four hundred years of Roman colonization, following Julius Caesar's landing in 55 B.C.—years which left such permanent and conspicuous vestiges on the face of England —have made little enough impression on her language. Recent as the memory of that civilization must have been when the Angles and Saxons arrived, they seem to have learnt nothing from it. A few towns, such as *York* (Eboracum), retain in a more or less corrupted form the particular titles given to them by their Roman founders, but outside these almost the only Latin words which we seem to owe to the Romanizing of Britain are *port* and the form of 'castra' (a camp), already referred to, which survives today in *Chester* and in the ending of many other town names such as *Winchester, Lancaster, Gloucester.* . . .

Then, during the fifth and sixth centuries of our era, the Angles and Saxons began to flow in from the Continent, bringing with them old Aryan words like *dew, night, star,* and *wind,* which they had never forgotten, new words which they had coined or developed in their wanderings, and Latin words which they had learnt as provincial subjects of the Roman Empire,[1] bringing, in fact, that peculiar Teutonic variant of the Aryan tongue which forms the rich nucleus of our English vocabulary. Their arrival here was followed almost immediately by their conversion to Christianity; and this moment in our history was a pregnant one for the future of Europe. For now the two great streams of humanity—Teutonic blood from the one side, and from the other the old classical civilization, bearing in its dark womb the strange, new Christian impulse—met. The Latin and Greek words which entered our language at this period are concerned for the most part with the dogma and ritual of the Church; such are *altar, candle, clerk, creed, deacon, hymn, martyr, mass, nun, priest, psalm, shrine, stole, temple,* and many others. Far more important was the alteration which now gradually took place in the *meanings* of many old Teutonic words—words like *heaven,* which had hitherto denoted a 'canopy', or *bless,* which had meant to 'consecrate with blood'. But to this we must return later, when we come to consider what is called the 'semantic' history of English words—that is to say, the history of their meanings.

Although Christianity did not come officially from Rome to England until Augustine landed in A.D. 597, it had already found its way here indirectly during the Roman occupation. Obliterated by the pagan Anglo-Saxons, it had continued to flourish in Ireland, and the actual conversion of most of the English is believed to have

[1] See p. 94.

been the work of Celtic Christians, who returned from Ireland and established missionary bases in Scotland and Northumbria. Their influence was so extensive that 'Scotia', the old name for Ireland, came to be applied to the country which we still know as *Scotland*. *Pat* and *Taffy*, the popular nicknames for an Irishman and a Welshman, are descended from the Celtic saints, Patrick and David, and it is interesting to reflect that the Celtic missionaries were starting their work in Northumbria at almost exactly the same moment as Saint Augustine landed in Kent. Thus Christianity enfiladed England, as it were, from both ends; and while the southern Anglo-Saxons were learning the Greek and Latin words to which we have referred, the Irish Christians in the north had been making the language a present of a few Celtic words, two of which—*druid* and *lough*—have survived. Again, although the name for the instrument of the Passion comes to us ultimately from the Latin 'crux', yet the actual form which the word *cross* has taken in our language is very largely due to these Irish Christians. But for them it would probably have been something like *cruke*, or *cruce*, or *crose*. This word has an interesting history. It was adopted from the old Irish 'cros' by the Northmen, and it is due to them that the final 's' took on that hissing sound which is represented in modern spelling by 'ss'. We may suppose, therefore, that but for the Irish Christians the word would have been something like *cruce*, and but for the Northmen it might have been *croz* or *croy*.

In the ninth and tenth centuries these Northmen, the Scandinavian Teutons, whom our ancestors called Danes, established an ascendancy over a large part of England. They seem to have mingled easily with the English, and we can trace back to their dialect some of the very commonest features of our language. Thus, the Scandinavian pronouns, *they*, *them*, *their*, *she*, gradually replaced less convenient Anglo-Saxon forms, and it is to the Northmen that we owe that extremely useful grammatical achievement which has enabled us to form both the genitive and the plural of nearly *all* nouns by merely adding the letter 's'. Other Scandinavian words are *call*, *get*, *hit*, *husband*, *knife*, *leg*, *odd*, *same*, *skin*, *take*, *want*, *wrong*; and there are many more hardly less common. The mighty word *law*, together with *outlaw*, *hustings*, *wapentake*, *moot*, and *riding* (division of Yorkshire) serve to remind us that the Danish ascendancy was no hugger-mugger affair, but a firm political organization. The old Anglo-Saxon words which these Northern intruders replaced, such as *niman*, 'to take', and *Rood* (the Cross) have mostly fallen out of use; but in some cases the two words survive side by side. Thus, our useful distinction between *law* and *right* was once geographical rather than semantic, the two words covering roughly the eastern and the western halves of England. Appropriately enough, it is a distinction which is much less clear in the German, and perhaps in other European languages than it is in our own. 'Recht', for example, covers both *law* and *right* in some contexts where we are obliged to choose one word or the other. The course of events, and the genius of the English language, seem together to have taken early cognizance of the fact that a separate name would be required for the thing peculiar to those who speak it, namely a rule of conduct which is enforceable by the Courts before it has been enacted by the legislature—a common or 'unwritten' *law*.

And now there followed an event which has had more

influence on the character of the English language than any other before or since. The conquest of England by the Norman[1] invaders brought about an influx of French words which went on increasing in volume for more than three centuries. At first it was little more than a trickle. For a long time the Norman conquerors did not mix much with their Saxon subjects. There are plenty of indications of this; for the languages, too, moved side by side in parallel channels. The custom of having one name for a live beast grazing in the field and another for the same beast, when it is killed and cooked, is often supposed to be due to our English squeamishness and hypocrisy. Whether or no the survival of this custom through ten centuries is due to the national characteristics in question it would be hard to say, but they have certainly nothing to do with its origin. That is a much more blameless affair. For the Saxon neatherd who had spent a hard day tending his *oxen, sheep, calves,* and *swine*, probably saw little enough of the *beef, mutton, veal, pork,* and *bacon*, which were gobbled at night by his Norman masters. There is something a little pathetic, too, in the thought that the homely old word, *stool*, could be used to express any kind of seat, however magnificent, until it was, so to speak, hustled into the kitchen by the smart French *chair*. Even the polite, however, continued to use the old word in the idiom 'to fall between two stools'. *Master, servant, butler, buttery, parlour, dinner, supper,* and *banquet* all came over with William, besides the names of our titular ranks, such as *duke, marquis, viscount, baron,* and

---

[1] These Normans, or *North-men*, were the descendants of a Teutonic Danish tribe, which had taken possession of Normandy about a hundred and fifty years before.

countess. The French word 'comte' was evidently considered to be equivalent to the one existing Anglo-Saxon title, *earl*, with the result that *count* never became an English rank. But since it had not been the Saxon custom to give ladies titles corresponding to those of their lords, the word *countess* was able to fill an important gap. That the Feudal System had an educative value and played its part in creating modern ideals of conduct is suggested by such words as *honest, kind,* and *gentle,* which meant at first simply 'of good birth or position' and only acquired during the Middle Ages their later and lovelier meanings.

Not the least interesting of the words that must have come over from France about this time are such courtly flower-names as *dandelion* and *pansy,* from 'dent-de-lion' (describing the ragged leaves) and the sentimental 'pensée' —remembrance. Many of these early Norman words seem to have a distinctive character of their own, and even now, after nearly a thousand years, they will sometimes stand out from the printed page with peculiar appeal. Perhaps this is especially true of the military vocabulary. That sharp little brightness, as of a window-pane flashing just after sunset, which belongs to the ancient, technical language of heraldry, such as *argent, azure, gules,* . . . sometimes seems to have spread to more common Norman words—*banner, hauberk, lance, pennon,* . . . and—in the right mood—we can even catch a gleam of it in everyday terms like *arms, assault, battle, fortress, harness, siege, standard, tower,* and *war.* The Norman-French etymology of *curfew* (couvre-feu) is too well known to require comment.

It will be noticed that nearly all these words are directly descended from the Latin, *beef* going back through 'boeuf' to 'bov-em', *master* to 'magister', *duke* to 'dux', . . . Thus already, by the thirteenth century, we can trace in our vocabulary four distinct layers of Latin words. There are the Latin words learnt by our ancestors while they were still on the Continent, such as *camp*, *mile*, and *street*;[1] there are the Latin words brought over by the Roman invaders, of which *port* and *Chester* were given as surviving examples; and thirdly there are those words—*altar*, *candle*, *nun*, . . . brought over by the Christian missionaries as described earlier in this chapter. These three classes are reckoned to account for about four hundred Latin words altogether; and lastly there is this great deposit of Norman-French words, of which the number must have been running into thousands. For it was not only terms of general utility which were transferred from one language to another. A second and entirely different kind of borrowing now sprang up—the literary kind. For two or three centuries Poetry and Romance had been making rapid strides in Italy and France. The medieval habit of writing only in Latin was dying out and Dante in Italy and Du Bellay in France had both written treatises extolling the beauties of their native tongues. French lyric poetry burst into its early spring blossom among the troubadours, with their curious 'Rose' tradition, and for two hundred years the English poets imitated and translated them as fast as ever they could. It was just at the end of this long period of receptiveness that an event occurred which fixed the ingredients of our language in a way they had never been fixed before. The printing press was invented.

A modern poet, looking back on that time, can scarcely

[1] See p. 44.

help envying a writer like Chaucer with this enormous store of fresh, unspoilt English words ready to his hand and an unlimited treasury across the channel from which he could pick a brand-new one whenever he wanted it.

> *Thou hast* deserved *sorer for to smart,*
> *But* pitee *renneth soone in* gentil *heart.*

Here are three Norman French borrowings, three fine English words with the dew still on them, in two lines. It was the May morning of English poesy.

For these were not 'French' words. Right at the beginning of the thirteenth century the English kings had abandoned Normandy, and the English Normans, separated from their brethren, began to blend more and more closely with their neighbours. In England French remained at first the exclusive language of the Court and the law, but, as the blood of the two peoples mingled, the Norman words which were not dropped gradually altered their shapes, developing various English characteristics, which not only differentiated from their original French forms the words already in the language, but served as permanent moulds into which new borrowings could be poured as they were made. *Gentil* changed to *gentle, pitee* to *pitie* or *pity*; and it was the same with innumerable others. Familiar French-English terminations like *-tion, -ty, -age, -able, -on,* were already nearly as common in Chaucer as they are in the pages of an average modern writer. Begotten on Latin words by generations of happy-go-lucky French and English lips, they were fixed for ever by the printing press, and today, if we want to borrow a word directly from Latin, we still give it a shape which tacitly assumes that it came to us through the French language at about that time. As Nature takes the human embryo through repetitions of its discarded forms—fish, reptile, mammal, and vertebrate —before bringing it to birth, so whoever introduced, let us say, the word *heredity* in the nineteenth century went through the instinctive process of deriving from the Latin 'hereditare' an imaginary French word, 'heredité', and converting the latter into *heredity*. It is usually done when we wish to borrow a new word from Latin.

We have borrowed so many that it has lately been calculated that as many as one-fourth of the words which we can find in a full-sized Latin dictionary have found their way directly or indirectly into the English vocabulary. A large number of these are Greek words which the Romans had taken from them. Thus, taking into account those Greek words which have come to us by other channels, Greek and Latin form a very large and a very important part of the English language. All through the history of our nation the two threads can be seen running together. At first sight they appear to be so inextricably twisted round one another as to form but one solid cord, but in reality it is not so difficult to unravel them. The fact, for instance, that *hospital* and *prison* are Latin, while *church* and *school* have only come *through* Latin from the Greek, is typical of the two main divisions into which the classical part of our language falls; for words which are genuinely of Latin origin—unless they have been especially used at some time to translate the thoughts of Greek writers—are very often concerned with the material outer world, but words of Greek origin are more likely to be landmarks in the world of thoughts and feelings.

Rome had spent herself in building up the external, visible framework on which European civilization was to hang; and this fact, observable in the word-relics of her military and political exploits, is observable still more intimately in the character and history of that great institution, our common law. Dignified vocables like *justice, jurisdiction, jurisprudence,* speak for themselves the lasting influence of the great Roman conception of 'jus'—that abstract ideal of the relation between one free human being and another in so far as it is expressed in their actions. It is not that in any sense we took over the Roman system; lawyers as well as poets are keen to insist that we built up our own. But as freedom slowly broadened down from precedent to precedent, there was always before the early English kings and judges a sort of pattern—more than that, a vital principle which had outlived one body and was waiting to be clothed with another. It was the spirit of Roman law living on in her language.

A whole chapter might be written on the numerous English words whose meanings can be traced back to the usages of Roman law. Take, for instance, the word *person.* Derived, probably, from an Etruscan word meaning an actor's mask, 'persona' was used by the Roman legislators to describe a man's personal rights and duties, which were defined according to his position in life. Its present meaning of an individual human being is largely due to the theologians who hit upon it when they were looking for some term that would enable them to assert the trinity of Godhead without admitting more than one 'substance'. When we remember for how long a time Latin continued to be the universal written language of educated

Europe,[1] the language of history and philosophy as well as of theology, we can imagine how the subtle flavour of this word's former meaning clung to its syllables through all their ecclesiastical soarings and was ready, as soon as it came to English earth, to assist the brains of our early lawyers in their task of imagining and thus creating that perhaps fortunate legal abstraction, the British subject. 'Obligatio' in early Latin meant merely the physical binding of someone to something; but in the Roman law of that date a defaulting debtor was literally bound and delivered a prisoner into the hands of his creditor. Thus, when a little later on this crude practice was abandoned, 'obligatio' came to mean the duty to pay—a duty which the creditor could now only enforce against his debtor's property; and in this way the general meaning of our word *obligation* was developed. Similarly *retaliation* came to us from the Latin 'Lex Talionis', the latter word being associated with 'talis' (such or same) and implying a punishment that fits the crime; while *advocate*, *capital*,[2] *chattel*,[2] *classical*, *contract*, *emancipate*, *formula*, *heir*, *peculiar*, *prejudice*, *private*, *property*, and *testament* are a few more examples of the same process, chosen from a great many.

Naturally many of these words came into the English language just after the Conquest. The French, being so much nearer to Rome, both in blood and in space, were a

[1] At least down to the fourteenth century. Even in Milton's time it was the language of international scholarship.

[2] Latin 'capitalis' from 'caput'—a head, and thus 'the status of Roman citizenship'. Under the old Roman law each citizen was assessed according to the number of beasts which he possessed. Thus, the word *cattle* is also derived, through French, from 'capitalis'. Compare the derivation of *pecuniary* from 'pecus'—a head of cattle, and *fee* from Old English 'feoh' (cattle).

century or two ahead of the Teutons in their civilization, and the Normans, after their long sojourn on the Continent, brought with them to England quite a complicated system of legislature and executive. Besides the Latin words to which we have referred, there are a large number of legal terms which are not so easily recognizable as Latin, having passed through Late Latin, Low Latin, and Early French colloquial speech before they reached our shores. In some cases they only developed a specifically legal sense in Late Latin or even Early French. Yet because the whole spirit of Roman civilization had been so impregnated with legalism, the capacity for expressing exact legal ideas seems to have remained latent, through all their curious vicissitudes, in such words as *assize* (literally 'a sitting down'), *court, judge, jury, county, district, manor, rent,* . . . Lawyers have gone on employing a queer kind of Anglo-French, in some cases, right down to the present day. The official use of 'Law French' in legal documents was only recently abandoned, and such technical terms as *champerty, feme sole, tort, chose-in-action, cestui-que-trust,* . . . survive to remind us of the days when an English-speaking lawyer would naturally write such a sentence as:

Arsons de measons felonisement faits est felony per le comen ley. (Arson of houses committed with felonious intent is felony by the common law.) The profession still sometimes refers affectionately to an old law-report, which mentions that the prisoner at the bar *jecta un brickbat a le dit Justice, que narrowly mist.*

Convey, felon, forfeit, lease, mortgage, perjury, plaintiff and *defendant,* on the other hand, have acquired a somewhat more general use; and indeed this Frenchified jargon, partly imported and partly built up by English lawyers as they went along, has produced in later times several words which the language as a whole would find it hard to do without. Among them are *assets* (French 'assez'), *burglar, cancel, conventional, disclaim, flotsam* and *jetsam, jettison, improve, matter-of-fact, mere,* 'the *premises*', *realize, size,* and— in its modern sense—*franchise;* while *culprit,* which was used in court down to the eighteenth century, has an interesting history of its own. In former days, when the prisoner had pleaded 'Not Guilty', the Clerk of the Crown would open proceedings by saying 'Culpable: prest', meaning that the prisoner *is* 'guilty', and I am 'ready' to prove it. In the official records of the case this formula was abbreviated, first to 'cul-prest' and afterwards to 'cul-prit', until later clerks formed the habit of running the two words together.

Looking at such words as *cancel, improve, realize,* and *size,* we can feel the force of Professor Maitland's remark that in the Middle Ages 'Law was the point where life and logic met'. It served another purpose besides that of establishing a secure polity; for through it some of the new Latin words which were gradually being created by its own, or translated from Greek, thought by the abstruse scholastic philosophy of the day found their way into the vocabulary of the people. Even the old word *cause* seems to have reached us by way of the law courts. They were thus the pipe through which a little of that hard thinking by the few, which underpins every great civilization, could flow into the common consciousness of the many, and in their terminology we can see most clearly an example of that never-pausing process by which the speculative metaphysics of yesterday are transformed into the 'common sense' of today.

IV

MODERN ENGLAND

SPORT · CADDIE · CANNIBAL · TORY · FINANCE

The English language has been facetiously described as 'French badly pronounced'. At the death of Chaucer, and for nearly a hundred years afterwards, this description would have been very nearly a true one. Apart from the adoption of a few Latin words, changes seem to have been few and insignificant during the fifteenth century, and we may assume that, for the first half of it at any rate, the Hundred Years' War was occupying too many of our energies to leave much time for cultural growth. Nevertheless, from developments such as those which have been pointed out in some of our legal terminology we can feel something of the way in which the genius of the English language was steadily, if slowly, reasserting itself and claiming its right to a separate personality. At the Reformation, when England finally shook herself free from the dangerous embraces of the Holy Roman Empire, the period of excessive French influence came to an end. The general effect of Protestantism on our language, subtle and profound as it has been, will be dealt with later, but the Reformation cannot be passed over here without recording one instance in which a word—perhaps a misunderstood word—has had extraordinarily lasting results. It is the confusion of the English *Sunday* with the Jewish *Sabbath*[1] and the consequent fastening upon that day of rest of many of the sombre inhibitions entailed by Sabbatic Law.

There is, however, another historical event which had a far more universal and direct bearing on English words, and that is the Revival of Learning. The new intercourse with the ancient literatures of Greece and Rome naturally brought into English a positive stream of 'literary borrowings'. At first these were mostly Latin words. If we try to imagine an English from which such words as *accommodate, capable, capacious, compute, corroborate, distinguish, efficacy, estimate, experiment, insinuate, investigate,* and a host of others equally common are as yet absent, we may partly realize what an important part was played by the Renaissance in producing the language in which we speak and think. There is indeed good evidence that the stream of new words flowed too fast at this time for ordinary people to keep up with it. For instance, many of the Latin words that were borrowed have since fallen out of use. At the beginning of the seventeenth century Francis Bacon, who is not a fantastic writer, was using such unfamiliar expressions as *contentation, contristation, digladiation, morigeration, redargution, ventosity,* . . . and somewhat before this, when the Classical influx was at its height, it was conspicuous enough to call forth several amusing parodies. We remember Shakespeare's Holofernes in *Love's Labour's Lost,* and Sir Thomas Wilson includes in his *Arte of Rhetorike* a fictitious

[1] First found with the meaning of *Sunday* in an edict of the Long Parliament.

letter applying for a church benefice, in which he satirizes as follows the Klondyke rush after fashionable Latinity:

'Pondering, expending, and revoluting with myself, your ingent affability, and ingenious capacity for mundane affairs: I cannot but celebrate and extoll your magnifical dexterity above all other. For how could you have adepted such illustrate prerogative, and domestical superiority, if the fecundity of your ingeny had not been so fertile and wonderful pregnant? . . .'

Now this outcrop of linguistic parody is significant for other reasons too. It reminds us that the English language had at last become 'self-conscious'. In former times the struggle between different ways of saying the same thing, between the old and the new, the native and the foreign, had generally worked itself out under the surface, amid the half-conscious preferences of the mass of the people. Thus, the old English translators who rendered the Latin 'exodus' as *outfaring* and 'discipulus' (disciple) as *learning-boy*, were not consciously trying to keep the Latin words out; nor did the fourteenth-century author of a book, which he called the *Againbite of Inwit*, have any academic horror, as far as we know, of the new Latin borrowings *remorse* and *conscience*, with one of which, at least, he must have been familiar. The same may be said of Wyclif, who translated 'resurrectio' *againrising* and 'immortalitas' *undeadliness*. These old writers anglicized because it came natural to them to anglicize, just as the next generation began to prefer the Latin words. But it was not so in Italy, nor in France, in both of which countries poets had long ago written careful treatises on the beloved medium of their art, their native language. And now, after the Revival of

Learning, in England, too, scholars and literary men began to notice such things. Counterbalancing the enthusiasm for Latin and Greek, there arose a 'Purist' movement of just the kind which has had such a powerful effect on the development of modern German. People tried to expel all 'foreign' words from the language; Sir John Cheke began a translation of the New Testament in which none but native words were to be used; and we find in his *Matthew* *moond* for *lunatic, hundreder* for *centurion, frosent* (from-sent) for *apostle, crossed* for *crucified, freshman* for *proselyte*, and many other equally odd-sounding concoctions. To look back in this way on the uncertainty and chaos which reigned at the beginning of the seventeenth century is to intensify our admiration for the scholarship and poetic taste displayed by the devout compilers of the Authorised Version.

If we were to look for another symptom of this sometimes pedantic self-consciousness, we could find it in the modern way of spelling *debt* and *doubt*. The old orthography, *det* and *dout*, is a perfectly correct English rendering of the French words from which they are taken, but the scholars of the Renaissance, anxious to show the ultimate derivation from the Latin stems 'deb' and 'dub', inserted an entirely unnecessary 'b' into the words, and there it has stayed ever since. Sometimes, too, these Elizabethan dons made learned howlers, as in the now abandoned spelling *abhominable*, which arose from a quite false idea that that adjective is derived from the Latin 'ab' (from) and 'homo' (man).

One can also get a curiously vivid sense of the way in which new Latin words had been streaming into the language during the sixteenth century from Bacon's literary style. He is so fond of placing a Latin and an English word side by side, in order to express what is virtually a single idea, that two consecutive pages of the *Advancement of Learning* supply no less than ten examples of this habit. Among them are *immoderate and overweening, action and business, charge and accusation, eloquence and speech.* To understand the exact effect which this kind of writing must have had on the ears of his contemporaries we must try to realize the faintly novel and difficult sound with which many of these Latin syllables would still be ringing. No such effort is required, however, to comprehend the way in which this deliberate duplication must have helped to familiarize English people with the sound and meaning of the new words.

Very soon the Greek language too began to be drawn upon, though never to quite the same extent as Latin. Thus, English of the fifteenth century must also be thought of as a language in which hundreds of familiar words like *apology, apostrophe, bucolic, climax, drama, emphasis, encyclopedia, epidemic, epilogue, episode, hypothesis, hysterical, paragraph, parallel, paraphrase, physical,* do not yet exist, for these are all examples of words which came in with the Renaissance.[1] The number of technical terms of art and literature is particularly noticeable, and it was now that the foundations were laid of that almost automatic system whereby a new Greek-English word is coined to mark each

[1] Two of the words quoted are first found, according to the *Oxford Dictionary*, in Sir Thomas More, one (*apostrophe*) in the text and the other in the title of his *Apologie of Syr Thomas More, Knyght*, 'made by him, after he had geven over the Office of Lord Chancellor of Englande'. It is not surprising that the creator of a European success like the word *Utopia* should have had a fine taste in real Greek words too.

advance that is made in science, and especially in technics. *Automatic* is itself an example, and it is hardly necessary to add *chronometer, dynamo, magneto, metronome, telescope, theodolite, thermometer,* ...

But though the stern lovers of their native tongue were thus hopelessly outclassed, yet the mere existence of the conservative feeling which they tried to voice must have acted as a useful brake on the too indiscriminate adoption of new words. The English language was, in fact, settling down. It was in the future to receive countless additions— never to change its very essence as it had done in the thirteenth and fourteenth centuries. And thus, as we look on towards the modern period, we find only fewer and more scattered historical vestiges. But if we can no longer expect etymology to tell us anything approaching to a complete and coherent tale, it will nevertheless still light up for us from different angles different little portions of that dark, mysterious mass, the past.

By the sixteenth century, for example, that peculiarly English characteristic, the love of sport, had already begun to make its mark on the language. *Sport* itself is an abbreviation of 'disport', a French word meaning 'to carry oneself in a different direction from that of one's ordinary business'. It is interesting to observe how both the form and meaning of the English word have diverged from their origin, and how they have since been reborrowed into French and most of the other languages of Europe. Italian tailors will even use the term to describe a roll of loud check cloth! Of the older sports, hawking has given us *allure, haggard, rebate,* and *reclaim*. The Latin 'reclamare' had meant 'to cry out against' or 'to contradict'; it was only in hawking that it acquired its present sense of 'calling back' from the cries that were uttered to summon the hawk back to the wrist. *Allure* is from the old *lure*, an apparatus for recalling the birds, and *haggard* is a word of obscure etymology which was used of a wild hawk. *Forte* and *foible* are old fencing terms, describing the strong and weak (*feeble*) points of a sword. *Couple, muse, relay, retrieve* (French 'retrouver'), *run riot, ruse, sagacious, tryst,* and *worry* we owe to hunting, as also the development of the Latin 'sentire' into the English word *scent.* Of these the most interesting are perhaps *muse,* which is supposed to be derived from the same word as *muzzle,* and *ruse,* another form of *rush.* The hounds were said to 'muzzle' when they sniffed the air in doubt about the scent, and a *ruse* was a doubling of the hunted animal on its own tracks. *Rove* (but not *rover*) is from archery, meaning in the first place 'to shoot arrows at an arbitrarily selected target'. *Bias, bowl over,* and *rub* in the phrase 'there's the rub' are from bowls, *crestfallen* and *white feather* from cockfighting, and *chess, check, checkmate, cheque,* and *chequer* come to us through the Arabian from Persian, the central word being a corruption of the Persian 'Shah mat', meaning 'The Shah (the King) is dead'. It is not so generally known that the varied meanings of *all* these words are metaphors taken either from the game or from the board on which it is played.

The more modern sports do not yet seem to have provided us with many new words, but there is a promising tendency to transmute some of their technical terms into lively idiom. In this way we can use, for example, to *sprint,* to *put on a spurt,* the *last lap, clean bowled,* to *take his middle stump,* to *skate on thin ice,* to *kick off,* to *tee off, one up,* . . .;

and modern games have also been instrumental in preserving from oblivion the odd old French word *bisque*, of unknown origin, which came over to England with the now nearly obsolete game of tennis, as well as the French-Scottish *caddie*.

When we hear a golfer use this word, when we hear a Scotch person ask for an *aschet*, instead of a dish, or see the queer expression *petticoat-tails* on a tin of Edinburgh shortbread, we are taken back to the close connection between the French and Scottish Courts which existed in the days of Mary Stuart. For *caddie* is a corruption of the French 'cadet' (younger son), whence also modern English *cad* and *cadet*; *aschet* is a form of the French 'assiette'; and *petticoat-tails* a corruption of 'petits gateaux' (little cakes).

Another phenomenon of history which is very faithfully preserved in the English language is our long-standing and not always creditable nautical relations with the Dutch. From the fourteenth to the seventeenth century Dutch sea words continued to trickle into the language, the fourteenth seeing the arrival of *bowsprit* and *skipper*, the fifteenth of *freight, hoy, keel, lighter, pink, pump, scout, marline*, and *buoy*, the sixteenth of *aloof, belay, dock, mesh, reef, rover*, and *flyboat*, while the seventeenth century, when Van Tromp nailed his broom to the mast, the Dutch fleet sailed up the Medway, and William of Orange sat upon the English throne, gave us *avast, bow, boom, cruise, cruiser, gybe*, and *keelhaul*. Besides these maritime words English possesses certain military memories of the Dutch. *Freebooter* goes back to the war with Spain in the reign of Elizabeth, and *cashier, domineer, drill, furlough*, and *onslaught* are also among the words brought back from the Low Countries by

English soldiers. A particularly freakish Dutch borrowing is the apparently English *forlorn hope*, which is in reality a popular corruption of the Flemish 'verloren hoop', a phrase that has nothing to do with hope and means a 'lost expedition'.

The Spanish words in the English language, like the Dutch, are few in number, but often full of history. Those which came originally from Arabic—the most interesting of all—will be dealt with in another chapter. We received them for the most part through the French. *Alligator*,[1] *chocolate*, *cocoa*, and *tomato*, which come through Spanish from Mexican, commemorate the Spanish conquest of Mexico, and *breeze* is a sixteenth-century adaptation of the Spanish 'briza', a name for the north-east trade wind in the Spanish Main. Of the other words which come to us through Spanish *cannibal*, *hammock*, *hurricane*, *maize*, and *savannah* are Caribbean, while *canoe*, *potato*, and *tobacco* are South American. *Cannibal*, like the names *West Indies* and *Indian* (meaning 'aboriginal inhabitant of America'), hides a more detailed history. It was brought back by Christopher Columbus, who believed, when he reached the islands of the Caribbean Sea, that he had sailed right round the world, back to the east coast of India. The name 'Caniba'—a variant of 'Carib' or 'Caribes'—he took as a proof that the inhabitants were subjects of the Grand Khan of Tartary.

We can see, then, how the new impulse towards travel and exploration which followed the Renaissance left behind, when it ebbed, many exotic and exotic-sounding words whose etymologies can tell us not a little of the nationality of those adventurous mariners who led the way

[1] A corrupted form of 'al-lagarto'—'the lizard'.

to the East and to the new world. The Spaniards were not the only explorers. The Indian words *coolie* and *curry* come to us through Portuguese; *banana* and *negro* reached us from Africa, possibly by the same route; and *cocoanut* is from the Portuguese 'coco', a bugbear or bogy—alluding to the nut's monkey-like face. *Drub*—once used only of the bastinado—is thought to be an Arabic word brought back by suffering Christians from the Barbary States. *Amuck*, *bamboo*, and *cockatoo*, come from Malayan through Portuguese, and *caddy* (the receptacle) from Malayan direct. *Moccasin*, *tomahawk*, and *hickory* are among the words sent back to us by the seventeenth-century English settlers in North America. *Taboo*, *tattoo*, and *kangaroo* came home with Captain Cook from the Pacific.

Meanwhile, the civil and political history of England has been growing steadily. *Political*, *politics*, *politician*, and *parliamentary* first appear in the sixteenth century, and *Cabinet Council* seems to have been introduced at the accession of Charles I. *Cabal*, one of the few Hebrew words in the English language, probably owes its familiarity to two historical events. It was applied in Charles II's reign to a small committee of the Privy Council, also known as the 'Committee for Foreign Affairs', which afterwards became the Cabinet; moreover, a little later on it happened that the names of the five Ministers who signed the Treaty of Alliance with France against Holland were Clifford, Arlington, Buckingham, Ashley, and Lauderdale. Their initials thus arranged spell the word *cabal*, which was humorously used to describe them. Another far commoner expression which dates back to the Civil War is the phrase 'the *army*'. It reminds us that we had no standing army until after the foundation of the Parliamentary Forces. *Cavalier* and *Roundhead* are words which carry their history, so to speak, on their sleeves. They were both coined as terms of abuse, and among other uncivil relics of the Civil War which have found a more extended application, *fanatic* and *Puritan* were invented by the Royalists and *malignant* by the Roundheads. *Independent* and *independence* are also Puritan words, and the useful *demagogue* first appeaerd in the *Eikon Basilike*, the famous pamphlet in defence of the Crown, which Milton answered with his *Eikonoklastes*. The expression *to send to Coventry* is probably a gift from the rebellious citizens of Birmingham, who, according to Clarendon, frequently 'rose upon small parties of the King's' and either killed them or sent them, as prisoners, to Coventry, which was a Parliamentary stronghold.

Spite, which always loves a rich vocabulary, is also the father of those venerable labels *tory* and *whig*. The old Celtic word *tory* was first applied in the seventeenth century to the unfortunate Irish Catholics, dispossessed by Cromwell, who became savage outlaws living chiefly upon plunder; after that it was used for some time of bandits in general, and at the close of James II's reign the 'Exclusioners' found it a conveniently offensive nickname for those who favoured the succession of the Roman Catholic James, Duke of York. Thus, when William of Orange finally succeeded in reaching the throne, it became the approved name of one of the two great political parties in Great Britain. *Whig* is a shortened form of *whiggamore*, a name given to certain Scotchmen from the word *whiggam*, which they used in driving their horses. It was first used of the rebellious Scottish Covenanters who marched to Edinburgh in 1648; then of the Exclusioners, who were opposed to the accession of James; and finally, from 1689 onwards, of the other great political party or one of its adherents.

That the seventeenth century saw the true genesis of many of our commercial and financial institutions is suggested by the fact that their names first appear at this time. Such are *capital*, which is a doublet of *cattle*—the very oldest Aryan form of wealth[1]—*commercial, discount, dividend, insurance, investment,* and lastly the modern meaning of *bank*, which, like the names of so many protective and responsible institutions—the *Assizes*, the *Bench*, the *Consulate*, the *Council*, the *Chair* at a public meeting, a *Seat* in Parliament, and the *Throne*—is based etymologically on what may well be one of the oldest and safest of human occupations. The old Teutonic word which subsequently became modern English *bench* was adopted into Italian, probably from the Teutonic Lombards of northern Italy, in the form 'banco'. It soon acquired the special sense of a moneychanger's 'bench' or table and found its way, together with the object it represents, into most of the countries of Europe. Thus, like the name *Lombard Street*, the little word carries us back with it to the origin of banking in northern Italy and to Edward I's substitution of Italian *bankers* for Jewish moneylenders. *Bankruptcy, currency,* and *remittance* appeared in the first half of the eighteenth century, and in the second *bonus, capitalist, consols,* and *finance*. The history of *finance* is again interesting. The word goes right back to the Latin 'finis' (end). When it first appeared in English, it had the sense of a 'fine' or forfeit, but its modern significance was

[1] See p. 60, note.

developed in eighteenth-century France among the tax-farmers or 'financiers', as they were called, to whom the king delegated the duty of collecting his taxes. As time went on, these shrewd individuals amalgamated into a sort of limited company, which, by a judicious application of the principles of usury, gradually gained more and more control over the revenue, until 'toutes les finances du royaume', as Voltaire says, 'dépendirent d'une compagnie de commerce'. In England the phrase *Bank of England* first appears in 1694, describing a body of individuals associated for the purpose of lending money to the Government; and about thirty years later this still (1953) outstanding loan began to be known as the *National Debt*.

From the beginning of the eighteenth century commercial and financial considerations seem to have played a steadily increasing part in determining the nation's policy. Horace Walpole is the first person known to have used *speculation* in the sense of buying and selling stocks and shares; and *budget* (a little bag or pocket) may owe its modern political meaning to a pamphlet sarcastically entitled *The Budget Opened*, in which his brother Robert's financial policy received some severe handling. *Prime Minister* also takes us back to Sir Robert Walpole, to whom it was applied with derisive innuendo, for it had in those days more the sense of 'Grand Vizier' or despot's tool. In the old-fashioned *nabob*, as a synonym for 'plutocrat', we have a memory of the latter days of the East India Company when the squandering of large sums of money in London, often rounded off a life of empire-building in Bombay or Calcutta. The dictionary suggests, however, that later generations of Anglo-Indians preferred to bring back with them less questionable impedimenta, such as *pyjamas* and *shampoo*.

The phrase, the *Rights of Man*, takes us back to the American Declaration of Independence. The borrowing of *aristocrat* and *democrat* from French, the French word *guillotine*, and the appearance in English of *revolutionize* and *terrorize* are enduring relics of the French Revolution, and the word *sectional*, which came in in the nineteenth century, is closely bound up with the history of France, for it is derived (together with the geographical use of *section*) from the division of France into electoral sections under the Directory. The military meaning of *conscription* goes back to the France of the same period. To the campaigns in the Soudan we owe *zareeba*, and to the Boer War the Dutch words *kopje* and *spoor*. The 1914 War has left us the anonymous *stunt* and *gadget* (small mechanical contrivance), and the French *camouflage*, and President Wilson's *self-determination* has probably been added to half the languages of the world, while the expressions *eyewash*, to *scrounge* (meaning to 'steal'), to *get the wind up*, to *go west*, and possibly to *swing the lead* (to be idle at somebody else's expense), are idioms which may or may not take a permanent hold. In the second European War the Air Force has shown itself more 'fertile and wonderful pregnant' in the field of vocabulary than the Army. But it is too early yet to say whether *stooge* and *stooging*, *kite* (for aeroplane), *gen*, *bods*, and the rest of them will rise above the status of slang.

A list of new words like *anaesthetic, galvanometer, morse, railroad, telephone, turbine, . . .* which appeared in the nineteenth century, would tell a full and fairly accurate story of its extraordinarily sudden mechanical and scientific development, but such a list has yet to be compiled. More interesting in many ways are the appearance of new metaphors and idioms, such as to *peter out*, to *pan out* (from mining), to *blow off* or *get up steam* and to *go off the rails* from the steam engine, and many electrical metaphors such as those mentioned in Chapter I. For new ways of doing are bound up with new ways of knowing and thinking, and the true story of the nineteenth century, as of every other century, is the story of its mental and emotional outlook. To this long and intricate story the rest of this book is devoted, but before passing on to it a few aspects of our subject, with which there is not space to deal fully, may perhaps be mentioned.

The light thrown by certain words on the social history of England, as opposed to her political history, is a clear and often a new one. To look up in the *Oxford Dictionary* such words as *blackguard, carol, club, morris, teetotal*, or a thousand others which seem to have no particular historical significance, and to read through the many illustrative quotations, is to take a wonderfully easy and intimate peep into the past; while the dates at which such words as *magazine, news-letter, newspaper, novelist, press*, or again, *callers, small talk, tea-party, snob, antimacassar*, . . . appeared, together with quotations showing the particular shades of meaning with which they have been used, are in themselves a little history of the English people. What could be more suggestive, for instance, than the fact that the adjective *improper* was first applied to human beings in the early fifties?

Words which are derived from the names of real individuals, as *bowdlerize, boycott, burke, derrick, dunce,*[1] *galvan-*

[1] See p. 152.

ize, mesmerism, morse, sandwich, tawdry, or fictitious ones, as *gamp, knickerbocker, lilliputian, quixotic, pamphlet, pickwickian,* are sometimes, but not always, historically interesting. Again, the place-names of England, whether of country villages or London streets, are heavily loaded with the past, but the subject is such a vast and disconnected one that it would require, and in the *Oxford Dictionary of Place-names* has received, a volume to itself.

The characteristics of nations, as of races, are fairly accurately reflected linguistically in the metaphors and idioms they choose, in their tricks of grammar, in their various ways of forming new words. It is, for obvious reasons, easier to apply this principle to other nations than to one's own; nevertheless there are a few such points which English people can observe even in the English language. The number of words and expressions drawn from sport is a phenomenon which has already been touched upon, and it is at any rate a question whether humour has not played a larger part in the creation of English and American words than in those of other languages. The French 'tête'[1] is humorous in origin, and there must be other French and Latin-French words with a similar history, but English has really quite a number of words in which humour has taken a hand. One way in which this comes about is the process known as back-formation. We realize the facetious intention when somebody invents from the noun *swashbuckler* a verb to *swashbuckle,* or to *buttle* and *cuttle* from *butler* and *cutler,* but it is not so well known that the same process (probably with the same humorous intent behind it) gave us such sober words as *burgle, sidle, edit,*

[1] See p. 142.

grovel, *beg*, and *greed*. One of the most interesting back-formations is the verb to *maffick*, formed from the supposed present participle *mafficking*, which was coined to describe the festivities that greeted the arrival in London of the news of the relief of Mafeking during the Boer War. The well-known humorous device of understatement is respon-sible for the modern meaning of *hit* and most of its syn-onyms. The notion of striking was once conveyed by the verb to *slay*; by Tudor times, however, *smite*, which in Old English meant to 'smear' or 'rub over', had become the commoner word. *Strike* itself in Old English meant 'to stroke' or 'to rub gently', and *hit*, which is now universal in serious colloquial speech, meant to 'meet with' or 'light upon'—'not to miss', in fact; just as to *win* ('not to lose') something means, or at one time meant, in the British Army, to *steal* it. *Blow* and *thrash* are both sly agricultural metaphors, and the present popularity of such slang phrases as *wipe*, and even *paste*, meaning to strike, and to *wipe out*, suggests that this pleasing and rather simple form of humour is still active in English word-formation.

But the number of these little etymological side-tracks is almost infinite. We might, for instance, ask ourselves whether the colloquial use of *chap* for 'individual' (from the Old English 'cheapen' to 'buy', cognate with *chapman*, *cheap*, *Cheapside*, . . .) is really the unconscious self-expres-sion of a nation of shopkeepers, or whether it is purely accidental; in which connection we should have to notice a later tendency to renew a faded metaphor by substituting the word *merchant*, and so on. But the truly scientific way of approaching this part of our subject is to study the various English words which have been adopted by foreign nations, and the meanings they have developed there.

These were few enough up to the end of the seventeenth century, but from then on their number and importance increased; and we cannot help being interested in them, whether on the one hand the foreigner has merely employed them in despair of finding any word in his own language adequate to describe the object or idiosyncrasy in question, or whether his adoption of them implies that he has also borrowed the things of which they are the names. In the first of these classes we should probably put *cant, comfort, gentleman, humbug, humour, respectability, romantic, sentimental, snobbism, spleen,* . . . ; in the second, *ale, beef-steak, gin, grog, mackintosh, pudding, riding-coat* (redingote), *roast-beef, rum, sport, sportsman, waterproof, whisky,* and various technical terms of sport such as *box, Derby, handi-cap, jockey,* . . .

To the second group also would belong our most important contributions to foreign languages—the political words. When we find *bill, budget, committee, jury, lock-out, meeting, pamphlet, speech, strike, trade-union,* . . . on the Continent, and realize that the modern meanings of European words such as *constitution, represent, vote,* or of Old French words like *address, majority, minority, motion, parliament,* . . . are derived from English, we feel ourselves in the presence, not so much of something peculiarly English as of something universal which England has been the means of bringing to earth. That vast theoretical terms like *liberty, equality,* and *fraternity* should be borrowed by England from France in return for *committee, jury, meeting,* . . . that the French *ideologue* and *doctrinaire* should be bartered for *utilitarian* and *experimental*—these facts have been taken to indicate a certain division of function in the economy of European social evolution, the Frenchman producing the abstract moral ideals and the Englishman attempting to clothe them with reality. And it may be that in such important loan-words as *club* and *freemason* and *sport*, but, above all, in *committee*—that boring but sensitive instrument for maintaining the balance as between individual and associative personality—we can perceive the Englishman's secret: his power of voluntary co-operation, and his innate understanding of the give-and-take it requires.

While we can hardly expect to see an undistorted reflection of ourselves in the first group of words mentioned above, yet the grotesque meanings which many of them have acquired abroad are interesting partly for that very reason. They enable us, if studied carefully, to see ourselves not only as others see us, but as others saw us. And from both groups together we can re-create, as Mr. Pearsall Smith has pointed out, something of the curious England which was 'discovered' about the middle of the eighteenth century by the rest of Europe, can rejoice with Voltaire in her atmosphere of religious toleration and personal liberty, and admire with Montesquieu her haphazard constitution; we can take back to our native France or Germany romantic and sentimental memories of *le 'lovely moon' des Anglois*, or, better still, delving farther into the past, we can stride across the Italian stage in our top boots and our *redingote*, a moody and spleenful English *milord*, liable to commit suicide at any moment.

Important as they are, however, we must not be misled by this little group of words into supposing that English is a language which has given away much. On the contrary, surveying it as a whole, we are struck, above all, by the ease with which it has itself appropriated the linguistic products of others. Like Autolycus, or rather like Bernard Shaw's Shakespeare, its genius seems to have lain not so much in originality as in the snapping up of unconsidered trifles; and where it has excelled all the other languages of Europe, possibly of the world, is in the grace with which it has hitherto digested these particles of foreign matter and turned them into its own life's blood. Historically, the English language is a muddle; actually it is a beautiful, personal, and highly sensitive creature.

PART II
THE WESTERN OUTLOOK

V

MYTH

L et us take two common English words, *panic* and *cereal*, and compare them etymologically; we owe both of them to the personages of classical mythology. *Cereal* comes to us from Ceres, the Roman goddess of corn and flowers, and *panic* is from Pan, a Greek Nature-god, who was regarded as the protector of flocks and herds. But here the resemblance ends; for not only is one Latin and the other Greek, but one is the name of an object which we can touch and see, while the other relates to that inner world of human consciousness which cannot be grasped with hands. Now it is important to notice that the *word* is very much more closely connected with the *thing* in the case of *panic* than in the case of *cereal*. Certainly, we are interested to know that one of our words for corn is derived from the name of a Roman goddess, but we do not feel that it has much effect on our own ideas about corn. We feel, in fact, that reflection on the word *cereal* will tell us something about Rome, but very little either about corn or about ourselves. With *panic* it is different. In that intangible inner world words are themselves, as it were, the solid materials. Yet they are not solid as stones are, but rather as human faces, which sometimes change their form as the inner man changes, and sometimes, remaining practically unaltered, express with the same configuration a developed personality. 'Human speech and human thought,' said the psychologist Wundt, 'are everywhere coincident. . . . The development of human consciousness includes in itself the development of modes of expression. Language is an essential element of the function of thinking.'

There was a time when no such word as *panic* existed, just as there was a time when no such word as *electric* existed, and in this case, as in the other, before the word first sprang into life in somebody's imagination, humanity's whole awareness of the phenomenon which we describe as 'panic' must have been a different thing. The word marks a discovery in the inner world of consciousness,[1] just as *electric*[2] marks a discovery in the outer world of physical phenomena. Now it was said that the connection of the latter word, in its Greek form, with 'amber' would be informative if we had no other means of determining the electrical properties of that substance. Words like *panic* are important, because we really have no other means of determining how the ancients, who lived before the days of literature and written records, thought and felt about such matters. Its derivation enables us to realize that the early

[1] There is as yet no satisfactory word in English to express quite what is meant. The German 'Weltanschauung' (world-outlook) is nearer to it. If, however, the word *consciousness* is taken not simply in its finite sense, as 'the opposite of unconsciousness', but rather as including a man's whole awareness of his environment, the sum total of his intellectual and emotional experiences as an individual, perhaps it may serve.

[2] See p. 17.

Greeks could become conscious of this phenomenon, and thus name it, because they felt the presence of an invisible being who swayed the emotions of flocks and herds. And it also reveals how this kind of outlook[1] changed slowly into the abstract idea which the modern individual strives to express when *he* uses the word *panic*. At last, as that idea grows more abstract still, the expression itself may change; yet, just as the power to think of the 'quality' of an article was shown to be the gift of Plato, so it would be impossible for us to think, feel, or say such things as 'crowd-psychology' or 'herd-instinct' if the Greeks had not thought, felt, said 'Pan'—as impossible as it would be to have the leaf of a plant without first having a seed tucked into the warm earth. *Hero*, which originally meant a being who was half-human and half-divine, is a similar descendant from Greek religion which could not be extinguished from our vocabulary without restricting our outlook.

As to the number of words which are indirectly descended from prehistorical religious feeling, it is not possible to count them. We can only say that the farther back language as a whole is traced, the more poetical and ani-

---

[1] Like *consciousness*, this word must be taken here in its very widest, metaphorical sense, as of a human ego 'looking out' upon the world through the windows of memory, recognition, the senses, etc., and of the cosmos which it 'sees' through those windows. It is obvious that the *outlook* of every individual will be slightly different from that of every other, also that there will be a great difference between the average *outlook* of broad contemporary classes, such, for instance, as learned and ignorant, artist and scientist, agnostic and Roman Catholic. The widest gulf of all is likely to be that between the average outlooks of different historical periods, and this will be increased if we are dealing with different races—such as, for example, ancient Egyptians and modern Americans—for in this case the dissimilarity will extend over nearly every experience of which the human *outlook* is composed.

mated do its sources appear, until it seems at last to dissolve into a kind of mist of myth. The beneficence or malignance —what may be called the soul-qualities—of natural phenomena, such as clouds or plants or animals, make a more vivid impression at this time than their outer shapes and appearances.[1] Words themselves are felt to be alive and to exert a magical influence. But, as the period which has elapsed since the beginning of the Aryan culture is only a tiny fragment of the whole epoch during which man has been able to speak, it is only in glimpses that we can perceive this; in a word here and a word there we trace but the final stages of a vast, age-long metamorphosis from the kind of outlook which we loosely describe as 'mythological' to the kind which we may describe equally loosely as 'intellectual thought'. To comprehend the process fully, we must build up the rest of it in the imagination, just as, from seeing a foot of cliff crumble away at Dover, we may set wings to time and call up the immemorial formation of the English Channel.

The English words *diurnal, diary, dial* are derived from the Latin 'dies' (day), while *journal* comes to us, via the French language, from the same word. These syllables conceal among themselves the central religious conception common to the Aryan nations. As far back as we can trace them, the Sanskrit word 'dyaus', the Greek 'zeus' (accusative 'dia'), and the Teutonic 'tiu' were all used in contexts where we should use the word *sky*; but the same words were also used to mean *God*, the Supreme Being, the

---

[1] We may compare, unless we are enthusiastic naturalists, the enormously different impression made upon ourselves by two such outwardly similar creatures as a cockroach and a ladybird.

Father of all the other gods—Sanskrit 'Dyaus pitar', Greek 'Zeus pater', Illyrian 'Deipaturos', Latin 'Juppiter' (old form 'Diespiter'). We can best understand what this means if we consider how the English word *heaven* and the French 'ciel' are still used for a similar double purpose, and how it was once not a double purpose at all. There are still English and French people for whom the spiritual 'heaven' is identical with the visible sky; and in the Spanish language it is even a matter of some difficulty to draw the distinction. But if we are to judge from language, we must assume that when our earliest ancestors looked up to the blue vault they felt that they saw not merely a place, whether heavenly or earthly, but the bodily vesture, as it were, of a living Being. And this fact is still extant in the formal resemblance between such words as *diary* and *divine*.

The French 'Dieu', with its close resemblance to 'dies', retains the luminous suggestion of *day* and *sky* very much more vividly than any of our words from the same stem, but we have kept the Teutonic form nearly intact in *Tuesday*. The fact that 'Tiu's day' came in as a translation of the Latin 'Dies Martis' (surviving in French 'mardi') also suggests that for the Teutons, alone among the Aryans, the supreme Father-God afterwards became their god of war; and this may throw some light both on their fundamental character and on the nature of the experiences which they encountered during the thousand odd years of their sojourn in the northern forests.

It must not be assumed that the 'ancestors' spoken of above are identical with the Aryans described in Chapter I. By the time of the dispersion the thought of 'sky' may have been quite separated in the average Aryan mind from the thought of 'God', or it may not have been. We cannot say; we only know that at one time, among the speakers of the Aryan language, these two thoughts were one and the same. It is impossible to fix a point in time, and then to cut a kind of cross-section, and define the exact relation between language and thought at that particular moment. This relation—and especially in the domain of religion—is a fluid and flickering thing, varying incredibly in individual minds, leaping up and sinking down like a flame from one generation to another. Consequently no two theories on the religious beliefs held by the Aryans in the third millennium B.C. are alike; and we are concerned here only with those modern words which are the product of Aryan religious consciousness at some time or another in its history.

They come to us, naturally, by different routes, a few by the south-eastern and any number by the north-western group. *Pariah*, a non-Aryan word which has come into our language from the East, derives its peculiar force from the age-old division of India's population into castes. *Ignite* is from the Latin 'ignis', which is derived from the same parent word as the Sanskrit 'Agni', the fire-god. In *magic* we have a reminiscence of the Persian 'Magi', mighty prophets and interpreters of dreams, of whom three were said to have found their way to Bethlehem; but unless it be in the modern trade-name *Mazda*, there is little, if any, trace in our language of the great Persian religion of Zoroastrianism, with its everlasting conflict between light and darkness, Ahura Mazdao and Ahriman. The meagreness in our language of these relics of Hindoo and Persian religion is again eloquent of the total separation of the north-western and south-eastern Aryans. The whole vast structure of

Eastern philosophy, with its intricate classifications cutting completely across our own, was practically a sealed book to the West until after the French re-established a commercial connection with India in the eighteenth century. Signs are not wanting, however, that the rapid growth of interest in this ancient outlook, which has taken place in Europe during the last fifty years, may enrich our vocabulary with some extracts from the ancient terminology, such, for example, as *maya*—the soul's external environment considered as being 'illusion', or as obscuring and concealing the spiritual reality, and *karma*, the destiny of an individual as it is developed from incarnation to incarnation.

To turn from these nations to a member of the north-western group, such as Greece, is, for the etymologist, like passing from an arid desert into a land flowing with milk and honey. *Panic* and *hero* have already been mentioned. *Iris* (the flower, and also the part of the human eye), together with the beautiful word *iridescent*, have come to us from the Greek goddess Iris, whose outer form was the rainbow. *Titanic* is from the Titans, huge earth-beings who rebelled against God much as did the fallen angels in Genesis. *Hermetically* (in 'hermetically sealed') comes to us from the Greek messenger god, Hermes, by a roundabout route (see Chapter VII); and in more or less common use are *aphrodisiac, Apolline, Asia, Atlas, chimera, daedal, Dionysiac, Elysian, Europe, Hades, harmony, Muse* and *music, mystery, nemesis, nymph, paean, panacea, phaeton, protean, satyr, siren, stygian.* The word *erotic*, from Eros, a Greek god of love, is an interesting example of the way in which the experiences of past civilizations evaporate into essential refinements of modern speech. Because of differences between Greece and Rome, which it took about two thousand years to work out on the stage of history, we are now able to make a fine distinction, such as that between *erotic* and *amorous*.

The true Roman god of love, however, though in the world of phantasy he still survives in his original form, *Cupid*, has only actually entered our language in the word *cupidity*. In the difference between the material associations of *cupidity* and the more imaginative ones of *erotic* we begin already to divine a fundamental dissimilarity between Greek and Roman mythology. Other words which come to us from Roman religion are *cereal*, *genius*, *fate*, *fortune*, *fury*, *grace*, *June*, *mint*, *money*, *Saturday*, *vesta*, the names of the planets, *contemplate*, *sacrifice*, *temple*, *Host* (from 'hostia', the victim which was sacrificed), *augury*, and *auspice*. The last two words take us back to the Roman custom of divining the will of the gods by watching the flights of birds. 'Aves-specere' meant 'to see birds', and we still have the first word preserved to us in *aviary*. *Fury* and *grace* are translations of Greek names; but in some of the others— especially *money* and *mint*, from the goddess Moneta—we behold the late reflection of a highly significant process. It is this: As time went on, Roman religious feeling quickly changed in two almost opposite ways. On the one hand it attached itself more and more to concrete and material objects, and, on the other, its gods and goddesses were felt less and less as living beings, and more and more as mere abstract intellectual conceptions. Yet these two changes were not really opposite, but complementary. For as the visible part of a goddess like Ceres became more and more solid, as she came more and more to be used simply as a synonym for *corn*, the invisible part of her naturally grew more and more attenuated. Thus, the mythical world was much less real to the Romans than it had been to the Greeks. It was more like a world of mental abstractions.

Soon there was a 'god', or part of a god, for every object and every activity under the sun, and when the empire was founded, each emperor, as he died, automatically became a divinity. Today the first two 'divine' emperors, *Julius* and *Augustus*, take their places beside *Juno*, the Queen of Heaven, in our monthly calendar. We may say, in fact, that by the time Christianity began to spread in the Roman Empire, Roman official religion had become divorced from feeling altogether, its dry bones remaining little more than a convenient system of nomenclature. Not that the new religion had no serious rivals; but the doctrines of Stoics and Epicureans, the Mystery Schools, and cults such as that of Mithras, had little historical connection with Roman mythology. Yet if Rome contributed no discoveries of value concerning the relations of human beings to the gods, it was perhaps for this very reason that she was able to concentrate more exclusively upon working out their relations with each other; and in so doing she created jurisprudence.

But in the later days of the empire, when this attenuation of the imaginative and supernatural element in Roman mythology had already gone beyond its logical conclusion, when Rome had absorbed the myths of Greece and Egypt and sterilized them both, the soul of Europe was stirring afresh in the north. Contact between the Roman tongue and that of their subjects, the Celtic 'Galli' in north Italy and beyond the Alps, had grown more and more intimate. Gradually there came into being a sort of hybrid Low Latin,

the father of modern French and the other Romance languages, which in many cases expressed Celtic notions and
feelings in Latin forms. So it was that new life came to be
breathed into some of the dead abstractions of Roman
mythology; but it was a very different life from the old
one. Thus, the old Roman deity Sors (Chance) had long
ago developed for the Romans into a purely abstract idea,
referring to the drawing of lots. But up in the north, far
away from the capital, the 'sortiarius' became a mysterious
teller of fortunes by that means. As the years went on, the
syllables softened and smoothed and shortened themselves,
until they became the old French 'sorcier' from which
'sorcerie' was formed, and so our English *sorcery*. It is
strange to think how far this word has travelled from its
origin; and in the work of a modern poet we find it travelling even farther, changing from a process into a sort of
mysterious realm:

> *Heart-sick of his journey was the Wanderer;*
> *Foot-sore and sad was he;*
> *And a Witch who long had lurked by the wayside,*
> *Looked out of sorcery. . . .*

It was much the same with 'Fata'. For the Romans themselves the old goddesses called the Fata, or *Fates*, turned
quickly into an abstracted notion of destiny. But contact
with the dreamy Celts breathed new life into their nostrils,
and 'Fata' in Late Latin became spiritual once more. The
sharp sounds were softened and abraded until they slipped
imperceptibly into Old French 'fée' (Modern English *fay*),
and so *fa-ery* and *fairy*. *Demon* is the result of a similar
metamorphosis.

Myth

Now in dealing with mythology nothing is more misleading than to compare the gods of different nations, assuming that those who have etymologically similar names meant the same thing to their worshippers. For instance, it has been pointed out that the name Tiu descends from a word which also developed elsewhere into Dyaus and Zeus, but to suggest that Tiu was the 'same god' as Zeus would have little meaning. And it is the same with the other persons of northern mythology, such as Thor, the thunder-god, from whom we have *Thursday*, or Wotan (Odin) who taught men language and gave up his eye in order to possess his beloved Fricka (*Wednesday* and *Friday*). There are many external resemblances, etymological and otherwise, between this Teutonic mythology and the mythology of Greece, but for the historical study of human consciousness it is the differences between them which are really significant. Here there is no room to consider either the resemblances or the differences, except in so far as they are preserved for us in the words we use. And we notice at once how small is the number of our words which refer to the Teutonic myths. Where relics still remain they seem to be either—like *elf, goblin, pixy, puck, troll*—the names of the creatures themselves, still used but no longer felt to exist, or else—like *cobalt* and *nickel*, the names given by German miners to demoniac spirits—they have lost all memory of their original meaning.

There are, of course, exceptions, such as *Easter*, from an old Teutonic goddess of the spring, *Old Nick*, from 'nicor', a fabulous sea-monster, and *nightmare* from the demon Mara, while the concepts *earth* and *lie* (untruth) may possibly have originated as the divinities Erda and Loki. But compared with the number of derivations from older myths these examples are practically negligible. There is an accidental quality about them, and few have entered very deeply into our language. The Aryan family was now growing older and more firmly knit. While Slavs, Teutons, and Celts were still uncivilized, their cousins, the Greeks and Romans, had already developed an elaborate culture. Had the former been left alone like the latter, their mythology, too, might in time have grown down into the language. But that was not to be. The great Aryan family did not lose touch long enough. When Rome came, and with her Christianity, the missionaries naturally assured the believers in Thor and Wotan that Thor and Wotan were not. And coming, as they did, from a developed civilization, they not only ousted the old Teutonic gods from the language, but brought with them a supply of ready-made Greek and Latin words, many of which—did they but know it—drew their peculiar shades of meaning from a pagan mythology which they held in equal abhorrence. The classical gods and goddesses faded so slowly into the thin air of abstract thought that the process was hardly perceived, but the Nibelungs and Valkyries, the Siegfrieds and Fafnirs of Teutonic myth, were doomed while they were still alive. Thus our fathers beheld the death of Baldur with their own eyes, and were awake during the twilight of the gods.

Of course, where the events of Teutonic myth and legend were associated with a particular locality, they have left their mark in the names of places. These, naturally enough, are found for the most part in Germany. In Great Britain— apart from *Asgardby, Aysgarth, Wayland Smith, Wansdyke,*

Wednesbury, and some others—the place-names that have come to us from pre-Christian religion are principally Celtic, and are usually found—like *Cader Idris, Cader Arthur, Arthur's Seat, Kynance Cove,* . . .—in Scotland, Wales, and Cornwall. Apart from place-names, *galahad* is a relic of Celtic legend which has found a permanent place and a modern usage in the language; and there may be one or two others. But not many. In England the whole Celtic nation and language died early out of the common consciousness, and it died even more suddenly than the persons of Teutonic myth. This explains the freshness and delight which many young writers of the last generation found in the language and legend of Irish antiquity. To resuscitate, as Keats did, the invisible beings of classical mythology was to dig down into the roots of our present everyday outlook; to take part in the Celtic revival was to feel that you were looking out on the world through an entirely new window —or at any rate through one which had not been cleaned for centuries.

We seem only to owe one English word to the Slavonic myths, and that is the unpleasant *vampire*, which was brought back from the East by travellers in the eighteenth century.

The general relation between language and myth is, as the word *myth* (Greek 'muthos'—narrative speech) suggests, almost unfathomable; but before leaving the limited Aryan aspect, which is all we have had space to touch on here, one interesting etymology ought to be mentioned, which has sometimes been taken to conceal the whole root and purpose of Aryan culture in the history of mankind. The Hindoos look back to a great teacher called Manu. Whether this individual himself, or his name, is historical or mythical is not particularly important. Hindoo sacred language and literature reveal at any rate a prehistoric *belief* among certain classes of society that Manu was the originator of their culture and religion. Now 'manu' is also their word for *man*; and about this word, as it appears in the different Aryan languages, there are two interesting points. The first is that wherever it crops up it bears the double meaning of 'human being' and 'member of the male sex'; the second that it is thought to be cognate with the root 'men', implying 'to think', which appears also in English *mind*, Latin 'mens', ... We have seen that to the external view one of the most remarkable characteristics in which Aryans differed from the races they supplanted was their patriarchal system. The etymology of the word *man* suggests the inner reason for this, for it hints at a dim consciousness among the Aryans that the essential function of the human being—at any rate of the Aryan human being—is to think.

And side by side with the conception of the human being as a 'thinker', we find an instinctive feeling that the human race is especially represented by its male portion. To the Aryan outlook, wherever we find it, the human being is *man*, and God is God the Father. What exotic matriarchies may have held sway before humanity began to worship logic and masculinity we cannot say, for our language throws light only on that tiny portion of humanity's inner and outer history which is the peculiar contribution of the Aryan races; and, in doing so, it suggests that, in spite of their tendency towards monogamy and a rigid family organization, the 'subjection' of women has its roots very deep in Aryan psychology. In this respect Greece and Rome differed but little in essence from India and Persia. The impulse towards a different conception of women, both in their own minds and in the minds of men, which has been giving an increasing amount of trouble to the European races for the last two thousand years, was really, as we shall see, implanted in the Aryan outlook by foreign religions.

VI

PHILOSOPHY AND RELIGION

PAPER · MYSTERY · IDEA · ANALOGY · ANALYSIS
LOGIC · QUANTITY · HERESY

The difference between Greek and Roman character, which is marked so plainly by the way in which Aryan myths developed among the two peoples and moulded the finer meanings of their languages, is evident in many other English words besides those which we can actually trace back to such myths. For instance, the Greek 'scandalizein' and the Latin 'offendere' both meant to 'cause to stumble', but for us there is a subtle difference between *scandalize* and *offend*; for while *scandalize* and *scandal* merely hint at the liveliness of an emotion, *offend* and *offence* convey a sober warning of its probable results. 'Discere' in Latin and 'mathein' in Greek both meant to 'learn'; but the substantives which are derived from these verbs have come down into our language, the one as *discipline* and the other as *mathematics*. Rome turned instinctively to the external, Greece to the inner world as a vehicle for the expression of her impulses. And just as 'learning' for the Roman gradually came to mean 'learning to be a soldier', so the ordinary Latin word for 'teacher' (doctor) is now applied most commonly to a teacher of physical health. And these two are not the only Latin words which have hurried out of school in this way. 'Magister', for instance, has exchanged the class-room for the police-court and left behind the Greek 'paidagógos' (pedagogue) to express the most schoolmasterish kind of schoolmaster that can be imagined. Perhaps the most significant of all is *school* itself. Words for 'teaching' and 'learning' among the Romans inevitably came to express unacademic ideas. When they did want a word for academic processes they had to borrow it, like 'schola', from Greece. Yet, curiously enough, the original meaning of 'scholē' in Greek was not *school* at all. What the Roman felt about the whole business of book-learning and disputing and thinking and talking philosophy is indeed conveyed to us clearly enough by the meaning of the Latin 'schola', from which we have taken *school*. But to a Greek all this had been merely the natural way of spending his spare time. 'Scholē' was the common Greek word for 'leisure'.

Now this insatiable appetite of the Greek mind for thinking and philosophy is a phenomenon in the history of the Western outlook as sudden and unaccountable as the appearance of the Aryan peoples on the stage of history. As far back as the sixth or seventh century B.C. we find, side by side with the popular Greek mythology, a developed and intricate system of philosophy—a kind of language and thought, in fact, which, as the labyrinthine history of our own tongue is enough to show us, could not possibly have sprung up in the night. And in their writings the Greek philosophers themselves allude to sources from which they may well have taken the seeds of abstract thought. References are made as early as Pythagoras and as late as Plato to the priestly wisdom of Egypt; and when we remember that the time which elapsed between the rise of Egyptian civilization and the birth of Homer is about as long as the period between Homer's day and our own, we need not be surprised. Moreover, we find some evidence of the debt to Egypt in our language. Two almost indispensable pre-requisites for the development of philosophy are the art of writing and something to write upon. It is interesting, therefore, to observe that our word *alphabet* comes to us, through Latin, from the first two letters in the Greek alphabet—'alpha' and 'beta'—which are themselves in the first place Phoenician words. Greek mythology looked back to Cadmus, a Phoenician, as the founder of the alphabet, and it is now believed that the Semitic Phoenicians did indeed bring writing into Greece, and that they themselves took it from the 'hieratic script' or priestly writing of Egypt. *Jot*, in the phrase 'jot or tittle', is an English form invented by the translators of the Authorised Version for the Greek letter 'iota', which is also of Phoenician origin. *Bible*, on the other hand, is from the Greek 'biblos', which meant 'the inner bark of the papyrus', and so 'a book'; and *paper* was borrowed by the Angles and Saxons from Latin 'papyrus', itself a transliteration of the Greek 'papuros', meaning an Egyptian rush or flag, of which writing material was made. Both these words are thought to be of Egyptian origin.[1]

[1] And linked with an Egyptian myth of the origin of the alphabet; for *Byblos* was the Greek name for the Phoenician city when the ark containing the fourteen pieces of the body of Osiris was cast ashore and rescued by Isis. I am informed by a very learned friend that the same word is connected—particularly through Etruscan—with the God Dionysus, who suffered a similar dismemberment.

External evidence tells us that already, a thousand years before the Aryans began to move, Egypt had mapped out the stars in constellations and divided the zodiac into twelve signs, and we are told by Aristotle that the Egyptians 'excelled in mathematics'. But if there was among the priests a 'philosophy' in our sense of the word, we know little of it—perhaps because truth, unadorned by myth, was regarded in those days as something dangerous, to be kept religiously secret from all save those who were specially prepared to receive it. This idea of inner religious teachings, guarded carefully from the ignorant and impure, survived in great force among the Greeks themselves, and we come across references in their philosophy to institutions called *Mysteries*, which were evidently felt by them to lie at the core of their national and intellectual life. Thus that hard-worked little English trisyllable, without which minor poetry and sensational journalism could barely eke out a miserable existence, has a long and dignified history, into which we must pry a little farther if we wish to understand how Greek thought and feeling have passed over into our language.

We have adopted from Latin the word *initiate*, which meant 'to admit a person to these Mysteries', and the importance attached to secrecy is shown by the fact that 'muein', the Greek for 'to *initiate*', meant originally 'to keep silent'. From it the substantive 'mu-sterion' was developed, thence the Latin 'mysterium', and so the English word. The secrets of the Greek Mysteries were guarded so jealously and under such heavy penalties that we still know very little about them. All we can say is that the two principal ideas attaching to them in contemporary minds were, firstly, that they revealed in some way the inner meaning of external appearances, and secondly, that the 'initiate' attained immortality in a sense different from that of the uninitiated. The ceremony he went through symbolized dying in order to be 'born again', and when it was over, he believed that the mortal part of his soul had died, and that what had risen again was immortal and eternal. Such were the associations which Saint Paul had in mind, and which he called to the imaginations of his hearers, when he made use of the impressive words: 'Behold, I tell you a mystery!' And it is the same whenever the word occurs elsewhere in the New Testament and in writings of that period, for it retained its technical meaning and associations well on into the Christian era.[1]

The first man—as far as we know—to call himself a 'philosophos', or lover of wisdom, was Pythagoras, who applied the label to himself and his followers. *Philosophy* among the Pythagoreans, with its emphasis on astronomy, geometry, and number, was still decidedly Egyptian; but gradually, from these starry beginnings, the Greek mind built up a vast, independent edifice of thought and language. The words that have come into our language directly from Greek philosophy are numerous enough, but if we were to add those which have reached us in Latinized form, and finally those words which are actually Latin, but which take their meaning from the Greek thought they were used to translate, we should fill several pages with the

[1] See also p. 125. The Temple scenes in Mozart's *Magic Flute* are a Freemason's attempt to depict the proceedings within an Egyptian Mystery School, and the opera itself is plainly a fanciful treatment of the drama of initiation. (Incidentally, the noises made by Papageno when he attempts to sing with the padlock on his lips are an excellent illustration of the possibly natural origin of the root 'mu-' in 'mu-ein'.)

mere enumeration of them. The list would spread itself all over the dictionary, varying from such highly technical terms as *method, homonym* and *noumena* to common ones like *individual* and *subject*.

Perhaps a more accurate term than Greek philosophy would be 'Greek thought', for Greek thinkers took some time to arrive at the distinction, so familiar to us, between philosophy and other branches of study such as history. The Greek word 'historia' meant at first simply 'knowledge gained by inquiry', and some of the words which follow are first found in the works of Hesiod and Herodotus.

Among the words which have come to us from earlier Greek thought are *cosmos*[1]—the name applied by the Pythagoreans to the universe, which they perceived as a 'shapely' and harmonious whole—geometrical terms such as *pyramid* (probably of Egyptian origin), *hypotenuse* and *isosceles*; many of the technical terms of music, as *chord, harmony, melody, tone*; of literature: *hyperbole, metaphor, rhetoric, syntax, trope*; and a host of common words of wider significance, such as *academy, analogy, aristocracy, astronomy, cosmogony, critic, democracy, eclipse, economic, enthusiasm, ethical, genesis, grammatical, hypothesis, mathematical, method, phenomenon, physical, poetic, politics, rhythm, theology, theory.*

[1] This word has been used by English writers in various ways—generally as a synonym for *universe*. Of late, however, there has perhaps been a slight tendency to differentiate it by making it mean the universe *as seen and felt by a particular individual or body of individuals*—'the cosmos of our experience'. This distinction appears to be a fruitful one and will be adopted here. As the words are used in this book, therefore, we should say that there is only one *universe*, but as many *cosmoses* as there are individuals. In this way the word *cosmos* becomes a sort of tool with which we can detach, and objectify for the purpose of inspection, the purely subjective *consciousness* or *outlook* (see pp. 86 and 87, notes).

Philosophy and Religion

Of those which were translated into Latin by Cicero and other Latin writers, and possibly by Greek schoolmasters in Rome, we may mention *element, essence, individual, quality, question, science, species,* and *vacuum,* together with most of the terminology of grammar, such as *adjective, case, gender, noun, number, verb,* . . . *Type* comes from 'typos', a figure or image impressed or struck—from the verb 'typtein', to hit or strike.

In a sense, the thought of the earlier Greek philosophers may be said to have reached its consummation, its very fullest expression, in the writings of Plato. Among the words which are first found in his works are the Greek originals of *analogy, antipodes, dialectic, enthusiasm, mathematical, synthesis,* and *system*; while he imparted a new and special meaning to many others like *method, musical, philosopher, sophist, theory, type, irony* (the name he gave to Socrates's peculiar method of simulating ignorance in order to impart knowledge), and, of course, *idea* and *ideal.* Before Plato used it, the word ἰδέα meant simply the form or semblance of anything. It is connected with 'idein', 'to see',[1] and when Cicero came to translate it, he had to use the Latin word 'species', which had a similar meaning, being connected with 'specere', 'to see' and 'speculum', 'a mirror'. Today *idea* does not mean to us quite what ἰδέα did to Plato; but tracing the whole history of the word, we can see how it was Plato who, by his creative use of these four letters, began to make it possible for us to get outside our thoughts and look at them, to separate our 'ideas' about things from the things themselves.

Thus, it was not only Greek words of which he was to

[1] See p. 20.

alter the meanings, nor only Greek and Latin words. *Love* and *good*, for instance, are neither Greek nor Latin, and *beauty* is only Latin remotely, yet the spirit of Plato really works more amply in them, and in a hundred others bearing on the presence or absence of these qualities, than it does in such specifically Platonic terms as *idea* and *dialectic*. Let us try and trace the origin of some of the meanings which are commonly attached to the word *love*. As in the Mysteries, so at the heart of early Greek philosophy lay two fundamental assumptions. One was that an inner meaning lay hid behind external phenomena. Out of this Plato's lucid mind brought to the surface of Europe's consciousness the stupendous conception that all matter is but an imperfect copy of spiritual 'types' or 'ideas'—eternal principles which, so far from being abstractions, are the only real Beings, which were in their place before matter came into existence, and which will remain after it has passed away. The other assumption concerned the attainment by man of immortality. The two were complementary. Just as it was only the immortal part of man which could get into touch with the eternal secret behind the changing forms of Nature, so also it was only by striving to contemplate that eternal that man could develop the eternal part of himself and put on incorruption. There remained the question of how to rise from the contemplation of the transient to the contemplation of the eternal, and, for answer, Plato and Socrates evolved that other great conception—perhaps even more far-reaching in its historical effects—that love for a sensual and temporal object is capable of gradual metamorphosis into love for the invisible and eternal. It is not only in the New Testament and the Prayer Book, in the *Divine Comedy*, Shakespeare's *Sonnets*, and all great Romantic poetry that the results of this thinking are to be seen. Through the Church and the poets to the dramatist and the novelist, and through them to the common people—there is no soulful drawing-room ballad, no cinema-plot, no day-dream novelette or genteel text on the wall of a cottage parlour through which, every time the hackneyed word is brought into play, the authentic spirit of Plato does not peep for a moment forlornly out upon us.

In the latter days of Plato's life there came to the 'Academy' where he taught a young man from Stagira in Macedonia. His name was Aristotle, and after he left Plato he became for a time the tutor of Alexander the Great. In spite of their proximity in time and space, the difference between Plato's method of thought and the Aristotelian or *peripatetic* system can hardly be exaggerated. While Plato had concentrated his intellectual effort on mapping out what we should now call the 'inner' world of human consciousness; starting from the point of view of ancient tradition and myth, and working outward; relating his thoughts to one another in accordance, as it were, with their own inherent qualities; and deducing the sense-world from the spiritual world; Aristotle turned to the acquisition of knowledge about the outer world of matter and energy—that is to say, that part of the world which can be apprehended by the five senses and the brain. The two philosophers were alike in their emphasis on the importance of cultivating immortality—or rather of 'immortalling' (for they used a special verb which we have lost), but otherwise there were few resemblances indeed. To Plato the soul of the universe had seemed inseparable from his own soul, and natural phenomena such as the revolutions of the planets had interested him rather as tangible, outward pictures of the life within that soul. To Aristotle the world outside himself was interesting more for its own sake. Plato had looked up to 'Ideas'—real Beings with an existence of their own, which stood behind physical phenomena rather than within them. Aristotle deliberately attacked this doctrine, maintaining that the Ideas were immanent; they could not have existed before visible Nature, nor could they have any being apart from it; and they could only be arrived at, he said, by investigating Nature itself. When Aristotle laid down his pen after writing the *Metaphysics*, the word *idea* had taken a long step towards its present meaning.

Thus in Aristotle's imagination the two worlds, outer and inner, met and came into contact in quite a new way. The mind was, as it were, put at the absolute disposal of matter; it ceased to brood on what arose from within, and turned its attention outwards. The result of this was, of course, an enormous increase in the amount of knowledge concerning the material processes of the outer world. But that was not the first result. For, curiously enough, the first result was a pronounced hardening and sharpening of the mind's own outlines. Struggling to fit herself, as into a glove, to the processes of cause and effect observed in physical phenomena, the mind became suddenly conscious of her own shape. She was astonished and delighted. She had discovered *logic*. The actual Greek word 'logic' (ἡ λογικὴ τέχνη) is first found with its present meaning in Cicero, but he is speaking of Aristotle; the thing itself and the technique of it was the invention of Aristotle, and it was Aristotle who first used the word *syllogism* in its modern sense.

Perhaps the most significant of all those words which are first found in Aristotle's treatise on *Logic* is *analytic*. Here is indeed a new word made to express a new kind of thinking. *Energy, entelechy, ethics, physiology,* and *synonym,* are further examples of words which, as far as we know, were actually created by Aristotle, while we owe *metaphysics* to the accident of his having treated that subject after ('meta') his treatise on *Physics. Axiom, category, mechanics, organic, physics,* and *synthesis* are Greek words which take their modern meanings chiefly from Aristotle; but his emphasis on the concrete and his constant gravitation towards a kind of knowledge which might turn out to be practically useful evidently made him a favourite with the Roman mind. Consequently many of his words have come down to us translated into Latin. Among those which we can actually trace are *absolute, actual, definition, equivocal, induction, instance, moral, potential, property, quintessence, subject,*[1] *substance, virtual,* and the grammatical term *particle*; of the plentiful number which have flown, more indirectly, from his mind we may mention *conceit* and *concept, deduction, difference, experiment, principle,* and *universal.* In *quantity* (a translation of the Greek 'posotes'—'how-muchness'—and seemingly formed by Aristotle on the analogy of Plato's 'poiotes', from which we have *quality*) we can perhaps see

---

[1] It is curious how many of these would-be precise terms have since reversed their meanings. For the adjective derived from *subject* see p.176; *virtual,* which was once allied with *potential* as the opposite of *actual,* is now practically a synonym for the latter term; and the Greek word from which *instance* is taken was originally an objection to an argument, not an example of it.

the beginning of that interest in the *calculable* aspect of the objects of the visible world from which the exact sciences have arisen. The human mind had now begun to weigh and measure, to examine and compare; and that weighing and measuring has gone on—with intervals—for twenty-three centuries.

Thus, Platonic philosophy fades from our view in the person of Socrates, proving by *analogy* the immortality of the soul of man and the soul of the world; and the fatal chill has scarcely risen to his heart when Aristotelian philosophy comes over the horizon, vigorously investigating by *analysis* the structure and composition of the body of man and the body of the world. Thanks to his friendship with Alexander, Aristotle himself had hitherto unparalleled opportunities for collecting information on every conceivable subject. Knowledge, often inaccurate enough, was garnered from the four quarters of the civilized world, old manuscripts were edited and compared, and, above all, Nature herself was observed in a way which was quite new. After his death his followers went on putting his methods into practice. Side by side with the weighing and measuring went naming. And so to the three or four hundred years which followed we owe a good deal of the technical terminology of our arts and sciences. It was at this time, for instance, that botany first developed into a science. Many of the names of our commonest wild-flowers can be traced back to writings of the period, and the following examples are all taken from the first half of the alphabet: *aconite, amaranth, balsam, balm, box, calamint, celandine, cherry, chestnut, chicory, germander, heliotrope, marjoram, melilot.* Moreover, nearly all the technical terms of botany are Greek, and though most of them, including the word *botany* itself, were created later, writers of this period may be said to have given the lead with such learned labels as *calyx, perianth,* and *gymnosperm.*

When we are 'dating' a word in this way, however, we must remember that only a fragment of the whole of Greek literature has come down to us. Thus we cannot be sure, because a flower-name first occurs, about the end of the fourth century B.C., in a writer of the Alexandrian period, that it was actually created by him or his contemporaries. *Anemone, asparagus, bugloss, celery, centaury, clematis, coriander, crocus, lily, medlar,* and *mint* all go right back to Classical Greek, while *petal* and possibly *spore* are botanical terms which were already in use. On the whole, the Alexandrians probably collected, arranged, and renewed the meanings of more words than they actually created.

This is even truer in the case of medicine. The *analytical* method of thought led naturally in Alexandria to the actual dissection of bodies, living and dead. Aristotle himself is still regarded as the founder of comparative *anatomy* (cutting up). and it was he who first used this word in its medical sense. The peculiar meaning of the word *empirical,* moreover, derives from a set of physicians who held that practice was the one thing necessary in their art. It might be thought that with this foreshadowing of modern 'methods' there would have been a great influx of new information and new terminology. In actual fact we find that the Greek words (and their name is legion) in the terminology of medical science were either created later by the different European peoples, or else they appear in the works of Hippocrates, a physician who was practicing in Athens and elsewhere before Plato was born. Among the words found in Hippocrates are the Greek originals of *arthritis, catalepsy, diarrhoea, dropsy, dysentery, epidemic, erysipelas, haemorrhage, hypochondriac, hysteria, nephritis, ophthalmia, paregoric, phlebotomy, phthisis, quinsy, rheum,* and *sciatica;* while the word *apoplexy* is particularly interesting because its Latin translation, 'sideratio', shows that it originally had the sense of 'star-struck' or 'planet-struck'. *Crisis* is Hippocrates' name for the crucial point at which a disease takes a turn for the worse or the better. It came to England with this meaning in the sixteenth century, and was gradually extended to cover first 'the conjunction of stars on which this "crisis" depended', and then 'any critical situation'. *Anaemia*, however, and possibly *enteric*, seem to have been first used by Aristotle.

The centre of all this furious intellectual activity was the city of Alexandria. Nor was it confined to scientific spheres; for the results of religious and philosophical developments which now took place in and around the cosmopolitan city in the north of Egypt were, if anything, more far-reaching than those of empirical science. Indeed, it was from this point in history that theology and science first[1] began to be two separate studies, science eventually following the lead given by Aristotle and religion brooding over the profundities of Platonic or neo-Platonic philosophy and saturating them with feeling. Between Aristotle and Plato is the great divide from which flowed in two different directions two

[1] The striking exception is the fifth-century philosopher, Democritus, who definitely foreshadowed the Atomic Theory and, in fact, gave to the word *atom* its modern meaning.

separate streams, as it were, of human outlook; and just as the
modern European, whether or no he possesses any genuine
scientific knowledge, can trace the general shape and method
of his thinking back to the former, so, whether or no he calls
himself a Christian, he must trace much of what he regards
as his ordinary 'feelings' back to the latter.

For the stream of Platonic thought was now to join itself
with other influences coming, for the most part, from
farther East. One of the few Egyptian words which have
come down into our language is *ammonia*. It is the name of
an alkali which was said to have been found near a certain
spot in the Libyan desert, where there was an Egyptian
temple to Zeus Ammon, and it will serve to remind us that
Alexander the Great must have been deeply under the
influence of the Egyptian priesthood when, in 332 B.C., after
his brilliant career of conquests, he went far out of his way
to visit this temple before founding the city of Alexandria.
We find, therefore—as might be expected—a strong Egyptian element blending with what was Greek in the thoughts
and feelings that began to ferment in the more enterprising
Alexandrian bosoms. And that is not all. A third influence
was added. In the third century B.C. a certain capable ruler
of Alexandria invited a body of Egyptian Jews to translate
the Hebrew Scriptures into Greek. The Septuagint, as it
was called, was so successful that Greek soon became a
recognized language of the Hebrew religion. Thus, the
Greek version found its way into the synagogues of Palestine, where it may well have been read by Jesus of Nazareth.

Without making a study of the Septuagint, it is easy to
perceive how passionate Hebrew meanings were gradually
imported into the cold and clear-cut Greek words, until

classical Greek had grown slowly into the 'Hellenistic' Greek of the New Testament. Seeking for words to convey such notions as 'sin', 'righteousness', 'defilement', 'abomination', 'ungodly', the Jewish translators had to do the best they could with noises which to Heraclitus and Plato had implied something more like 'folly', 'integrity', 'dirt', 'objectionable practice', 'ignorant', Any number of such examples could be found. The harmless Greek word 'eidōlon' (*idol*), which had formerly meant any sort of mental image, including a mere mental fancy, suddenly found itself selected from its fellows to be spit upon and cast into outer darkness. 'Paradeisos', on the other hand— the park of a Persian nobleman—was spirited away, as though by the four Djinns of Arabian legend, first to the Garden of Eden and then to the heavens. It may well be that in the Septuagint version of the Old Testament, more than anywhere else, is crystallized out for us that process which went on in and about Alexandria for three or four hundred years, and which remained almost unaffected by the inclusion of the city within the Roman Empire. Language never ceases growing, but an important document such as this is like a cross-section of its stem. In it we can see clearly what an enormous part that Alexandrian mingling of Jewish, Egyptian, and Greek conceptions of the Almighty has played in determining the subtler part of the words we use every day—in building up those delicate associations of which few of us ever become fully conscious, but which we all instinctively bring into play when we are speaking under the influence of emotion.

And later, in the work of a writer like Philo the Jew, who lived and wrote about A.D. 50, we can discern some of the

religious activities which had followed the translation of
the Septuagint; how the Jew, with his instant expectation
of the Messiah, the Egyptian devotee, with his reverence
for Horus—the child of a virgin mother, Isis—who died
and rose again as the sun-god Osiris, and the Greek, with
his elaborated Platonic doctrine, met together, speaking
Greek; how innumerable sects, ascetic and licentious, philosophical and superstitious, wise and foolish, had been springing up and dying down all over the Alexandrian world—
all of them, to whatever extravagant lengths they may have
carried their philosophies and their dreams, working un-
consciously at the long task of altering the meaning, the
emotional colour, the evocative power of common Greek
words. Concepts such as 'God', 'world', 'love', 'soul',
'life', 'death', 'spirit', 'self', and a hundred others were
first resolved by the chemical action upon them of similar
concepts from the minds of other nations and races, and
then they began to be built up anew and to take on the
form in which they are presented, as he learns to speak, to
the modern European child.

Greek philosophy had developed in many directions
since Plato's day. We hear of *Cynics, Sceptics, Epicureans,
Stoics*, all of which words originated as the names of different schools of philosophy. The last two, whose doctrines
were to take such a firm hold on the educated classes of
imperial Rome, have given us one or two important words.
Apart from their moral teachings, they appear to have
directed their philosophical inquiries more especially to the
point of contact between thoughts and things or, as we
should say, between objective and subjective. 'Phantasia',
from which we have *fantasy* and *fancy*, was a popular word

with the Stoics, who gave it much of its modern meaning; *notion* and *comprehension* are Cicero's translations of Stoic terms; while *image* in the sense of 'mental image' and *spectre* are Latin renderings of Epicurean expressions. Epicurus had founded his doctrines on those of Democritus, and these last two words were employed by Cicero and one of his friends in discussing that philosopher's odd theory of perception. He had held that the surfaces of all objects are continually throwing off 'images'—a kind of films or husks which float about in space and at last penetrate to the mind through the pores of the body. Both the Stoic 'phantasia' and this Democritan word 'eidōlon', which Cicero translated by 'imago', seem to have contributed a part of their meaning to the later 'imaginatio', from which, of course, we have taken our *imagination*.

It was the Stoics, too, who gradually burdened the little Greek word 'logos' with the weight of a whole metaphysical theory of the relation between spirit and matter. 'Logos' in Greek had always meant both 'word' (an expressed meaning) and the creative faculty in human beings—'Reason', as it is often translated—which expresses itself by making and using words. The Stoics were the first to identify this human faculty with that divine Mind (Nous) which earlier Greek philosophers had perceived as pervading the visible universe. They were the first to make the progressive incarnation of thought in audible sound a part of the creative working of God in the world; and it is to them accordingly, with their deep sense of the divine significance of words and their origin, that we owe the word *etymology*, the first half of which is composed of a poetical Greek adjective meaning 'true'. Though he had never heard of Christianity, Philo, importing into the theory a certain Semitic awfulness, actually called this mysterious 'logos' the 'only-begotten-son'.

It must not be imagined that the majority of Alexandrian citizens were interested in these matters. Israel and Egypt resembled Greece in this, that they had in the first place their inner religious traditions, and in the second their stock of popular myth and legend. And just as, in Athens, the average citizen had accepted the teachings of ordinary Greek mythology, without knowing anything at all about the thoughts of contemporary philosophy, so was it in Alexandria, where the majority lived a life of easy-going frivolity and dissipation, paying to the gods the regular outward observances demanded by the calendar, and otherwise not bothering to think much about them until they were frightened or ill. Throughout the course of history the many have accepted, as far as they were able, the thoughts which have been made for them by the few in the past, and the few have gone on constructing the opinion of the future.

In Palestine Jesus of Nazareth lived and taught and died. As the years passed by, an increasing number of sages and religious teachers began to agree among themselves that recently something had actually occurred which had before only been talked about or erroneously believed to have occurred. Certain of the Jews, for instance, admitted that their Messiah had now come and gone. Egyptians and followers of the Egyptian cults were persuaded that a real Horus had been born of a virgin, and had risen again as an Osiris. Some of the more forward-looking among those who had been initiated into the Mysteries felt that what had

so often been enacted dramatically within the sacred pre-
cincts had now taken place in a peculiar way on the great
stage of the world, this time not for a few, but for all to see.
A God had himself died in order to rise again to eternal life.
Thus, those who had not been initiated—the poorer classes,
most of the women, and the slaves—had a joyous feeling
that at last the Mysteries had been revealed, that 'many
things which were hid had been made plain'. And some
students of Platonic philosophy could admit that this might
be true, that henceforth those who could not rise to the contemplation of the eternal in Nature might yet win immortality by contemplating the life and death of Jesus. For they
could see in Christ one who had first taught in a new and
simpler way, and had then Himself demonstrated, a truth
which nearly every one of the Greek philosophers, including Aristotle, had been trying to say all their lives—that, in
order to achieve immortality, it is necessary to 'die' to this
world of the senses and the appetites, and that he who thus
'dies' is already living in eternity during his bodily life and
will continue to do so after his bodily death. 'Whosoever
shall lose his life shall find it.' In the Christ the Logos of
Philo and his school had become incarnate in human form,
the Word had been made Flesh.

Such were some of the numerous ideas and emotions
which had become embedded in the Greek language by the
time that, somewhere about a hundred years after His
death, the life of Christ was written by the four Evangelists
and others. Out of these ideas and emotions arose, in the
first place, the dogma and ritual of the Catholic Church,
and in the second place a great part of the ordinary thoughts
and feelings and impulses of will which flourish in the

bosoms of modern Europeans and Americans.

Very early in its career the leaders of the infant Church must have realized two things—firstly, that those who, like the Gnostics, were passionately interested in philosophical and mystical interpretations of the life of Christ, not only differed very widely among themselves, but also often paid little attention to that personal life of Jesus, as recorded in the Gospels, whose sweetness was beginning to bind men together with marvellous new ties; secondly, that the simple and ignorant people to whom, according to the Gospels, Jesus addressed Himself almost exclusively, would be quite incapable of grasping these interpretations. If Christianity was to spread, it must be simplified. For these reasons the leading spirits gradually set their faces more and more rigidly against those long and laboriously evolved ideas which had actually created the language of the Gospels. And no doubt there were other reasons too: the most shocking immorality was rampant everywhere, and in those days opinion and behaviour were more closely bound up with one another. Moreover, in all but the strongest natures an extreme love of moral purity is often accompanied by an extreme love of exerting authority.

Therefore incredibly industrious Fathers busied themselves in editing and selecting from the literature and traditions of a hundred semi-Christian sects. Doctrines which had taken a very strong hold on many imaginations were accepted, given the orthodox stamp, and incorporated in the canon; others were rejected, and, being pursued at first with a mixture of genuine logic, misrepresentation, and invective, and, as the Church grew stronger, with active persecution, gradually vanished away or dwindled down to obscure apocryphal manuscripts, some of which have only been partially translated within the last few decades. Thus, for more than ten centuries, creeds and dogmas, to the accompaniment of immense intellectual and physical struggles, were petrified into ever clearer and harder forms. Christianity became identified with Catholic doctrine, and, soon after the Church's authority was backed by that of the Roman Empire, any other form of it might be punished by death. The stigma which still attaches to the ordinary Greek word for 'choosing' (*heresy*) is a fair indication of the zeal with which the early Popes and Bishops set about expunging from the consciousness of Christendom all memory of its history and all understanding of its external connections; while their success may be judged from the fact that as late as the last century an Englishman of public position who should have openly interpreted the Old Testament as Origen, for instance, interpreted it in the third century, would have incurred serious disabilities.

Consequently it is not surprising if we have found ourselves digging in somewhat unfamiliar places. Later on, the Catholic outlook spanned the whole imagination of the Middle Ages like the vaulted nave of a vast cathedral. By laying bare some of the foundations of that outlook and applying to them a little knowledge of the histories of words and their meanings, we can do something which we could hardly do else but by a long and difficult study of the arcana of the Dark Ages, their Neoplatonism, their monastic traditions, their Schools, and their cults of the Virgin. We can, in some degree, be present with our own imaginations at the building of the cathedral. And this is worth while, not only for its own sake, but because, as that huge edifice slowly ruined, we filched its worn but shapely stones and began to build up with them those bridges of feeling which join us today to our husbands and our wives, our children, our lovers, our friends.

VII

DEVOTION

PASSION · LADY · LOVE-LONGING · CONSCIENCE
INQUISITION · AUTHORITY · INDIVIDUAL · INFLUENCE

Plato, following the doctrines of Timaeus and Pythagoras, taught also a moral and intellectual system of doctrine, comprehending at once the past, the present, and the future condition of man. Jesus Christ divulged the sacred and eternal truths contained in these views to mankind, and Christianity, in its abstract purity, became the exoteric expression of the esoteric doctrines of the poetry and wisdom of antiquity. The incorporation of the Celtic nations with the exhausted population of the south, impressed upon it the figure of the poetry existing in their mythology and institutions. The result was a sum of the action and reaction of all the causes included in it; for it may be assumed as a maxim that no nation or religion can supersede any other without incorporating into itself a portion of that which it supersedes. The abolition of personal and domestic slavery, and the emancipation of women from a great part of the degrading restraints of antiquity, were among the consequences of these events.

. . . The freedom of women produced the poetry of sexual love. Love became a religion, the idols of whose worship were ever present. It was as if the statues of Apollo and the Muses had been endowed with life and motion, and had walked forth among their worshippers; so that the earth became peopled by the inhabitants of a diviner world. The familiar appearance and proceedings of life became wonderful and heavenly, and a paradise was created as out of the wrecks of Eden. And as this creation itself is poetry, so its creators were poets; and language was the instrument of their art: *Galeotto fù il libro, e chi lo scrisse.*—SHELLEY: *A Defence of Poetry.*

Apuleius and other imperial writers have left us a picture, gaudy and fascinating enough, of the earlier centuries of the Roman Empire. In their works the pomps and frivolities of that decaying world pass in procession before our eyes; the tenuous old Roman gods and goddesses rub shoulders in the popular imagination, on the one hand, with powerful relics of the Egyptian Mysteries, and on the other—already in the second century —with full-blooded medieval witches and demons; while the polite scepticism and graceful dissipation of the educated raises its eyebrows and shrugs its shoulders at the credulous fervours of Christians and their numerous fellow-cranks. There are only one or two common English words which throw any direct light on this period. *Martyr*, the Greek word for a 'witness', and so 'a witness to the truth', tells its story of the earlier days of the Church, as *heresy* of the later. The name *Constantinople* has a double historical significance. It bears the name of the first Roman emperor who recognized Christianity as the established religion of the empire, and it marks the removal in A.D. 330 of the imperial capital from Italy to the shores of the Bosphorus. That removal foreshadowed the inevitable splitting up of the Roman Empire into an eastern and a western half, a schism which survives formally today in the difference between the Greek Orthodox and the Roman Catholic Church. It may be called the starting-point of European history.

Huge shadowy movements were taking place deep down in the wills and imaginations of men. Powerful movements; for now the meanings and associations of all those

Latin words which were subsequently to come into our language in the various ways described in Chapter III were being built up or altered, not only by outstanding figures such as Saint Jerome and Saint Augustine, and the lawyer Emperor Justinian, but also by insignificant Roman legionaries and barbarian private soldiers, by outlandish scholars and studious, dreaming monks. In particular, an increasing number of the profound and manifold concepts which had been laboriously worked into the Greek language in the manner suggested in the last chapter were gradually decanted, either by actual translation or by more indirect methods, into Latin syllables. Thus, side by side with the Septuagint, there came into being the Vulgate, a Latin translation of the Old and New Testaments, finished by Saint Jerome in A.D. 405, and still the received text of the Roman Catholic Church. But it did not stand alone like the Septuagint. Many volumes of ecclesiastical literature are extant through which we could trace the gradual importation into the Latin language of the new meanings. For example, at the end of the second century—no doubt with the object of distinguishing the Christian Mystery of incarnation, death, and rebirth from its many rivals—Tertullian fixed the Latin 'sacramentum' as the proper translation of 'musterion' instead of 'mysterium', which would probably have disappeared altogether had not Jerome restored it to partial use. Thus one word, as is often the case, split up into two, *sacrament* remaining within the Church to express, among other things, part of the old technical meaning of *mystery*, while *mystery* itself, freed from one half of its associations, moved outside and quickly grew wider and vaguer. 'Passio', the Latin word for *suffering*, used in ecclesiastical literature for the death of Jesus on the cross, gradually extended in a similar way the scope of its pregnant new meaning, and we find already in Tertullian a derivative 'compassio'. From Latin, largely through French, such new meanings found their way into English, and it was these, as we shall see, more than anything else which transformed the country between the Norman Conquest and the fifteenth century into something like the England which we know today.

For if we omit the Dark Ages, and, turning suddenly from the civilization of classical Greece and Rome, raise the curtain on, say, thirteenth-century England, we are struck by a remarkable transformation. An attempt has been made in previous chapters to trace the general changes of meaning in certain key-words of human thought and feeling, such as *God* and *love*, *life* and *death*, *heaven* and *hell*, . . . When we reach medieval Europe, it is necessary to add a new class of key-word altogether. Let us look at a fifteenth-century English carol:

> *I sing of a maiden*
> *That is makeless;*[1]
> *King of all kings*
> *To her son she ches.*[2]
>
> *He came al so still*
> *There his mother was,*
> *As dew in April*
> *That falleth on the grass.*
>
> *He came al so still*
> *To his mother's bour,*

[1] Matchless. [2] Chose.

Devotion

As dew in April
  That falleth on the flour.

He came al so still
  There his mother lay,
As dew in April
  That falleth on the spray.

Mother and maiden
  Was never none but she;
Well may such a lady
  Goddes mother be.

In such a poem we have once more a kind of cross-section of the growth of European outlook. Between its lines we seem to be able to hear, as in a dream, the monotonous intonings of Egyptian priests, the quiet words of Socrates in the Academy, and the alert speculative hum of the Alexandrian world. It is so graceful that for the moment it seems as though all these things, with all the pillages and massacres and crucifixions and vast imperial achievements of Rome, had been conspiring together merely to load the homely old Teutonic word 'loaf-kneader' with new semantic significance, to transform it into that mystery and symbol in the imaginations of men, a *lady*.

The medieval lyric, as it gradually loses its exclusive preoccupation with ecclesiastical subjects, becomes more and more concerned with woman, and concerned with her in a new way. Through the poetry of Italy, where the Renaissance was already stirring, the troubadour literature of France, and that strange 'Rose' tradition which is preserved to us in Chaucer's translation of the *Roman de la Rose*, there grew up during the thirteenth and fourteenth centuries a small special vocabulary defining the landmarks in that new region of the imagination which the poets, and even the scholars, of Europe were just discovering; we might call it the region of devotional love. Indeed, it was more than a vocabulary; it developed at one time into a sort of miniature mythology, for the various conflicting elements in a lady's disposition which the lover had to meet with and overcome were actually personified, 'Danger' being a kind of mixture of modesty and haughtiness —an ill-omened creature whom 'Pity' or 'Mercy', if the lover was fortunate, finally put to rout:

> *Al founde they Daunger for a tyme a lord,*
> *Yet Pitee, thurgh his stronge gentle might*
> *Foryaf[1] and made Mercy passen Ryght.*

In these three lines from Chaucer's *Legend of Good Women* the four Anglo-French words *Danger*, *Pity*, *Gentle*, and *Mercy* are all Latin terms whose forms had altered, and whose meanings had received the Christian stamp during the Dark Ages. *Pity* comes from 'pietas' (compare *piety*); *gentle* from 'gentilis' meaning 'of the same family' and later 'of noble birth'; and *mercy* from 'merces', 'a reward', then 'a reward in heaven for kindness displayed on earth'. None of them—with the exception of *mercy* in its theological sense—are known to have been used in English before the thirteenth century. *Anguish, beauty, bounty, charity, comfort, compassion, courtesy, delicate, devotion, grace, honour, humble, passion, patience, peace, purity, tender* are further examples of this new vocabulary of tenderness which came to us from Latin through Early French. Some

---

[1] Forgave.

of them, such as *charity*, *delicate*, and *passion*, were probably
brought to England by the preaching friars before the
Conquest; others came with the devout Normans, and did
not develop a secular meaning until after they had reached
our shores (*devotion* remaining purely theological until as
late as the sixteenth century); while yet a third class had
already been secularized by nimble spirits like Petrarch and
Ronsard a century or two before they reached us by the
Norman route along with more frivolous terms, *amorous*,
dainty, *dalliance*, *debonair*, *delight*, *pleasure*, *pleasance*, and the
like, in which there is no particular reason to perceive a
strong ecclesiastical influence. All of them, apart from the
last group, are alike in that they started with a theological
meaning and subsequently developed an affectionate one
alongside of it. We may think of them as gifts presented to
the lyric lover by the Bride of Christ—well-chosen gifts;
for were they not the ardent creations of her own early
passion?

Thus, side by side with such lyrics as the carol quoted
above, we find in the Middle Ages charming little secular
poems almost indistinguishable from them in tone and
manner:

> *Sweet rose of vertew and of gentilness,*
> *Delightsome lily of everie lustyness,*
> > *Richest in bountie and in bewtie clear,*
> > *And everie vertew that is wened dear,*
> *Except onlie that ye are mercyless.*
>
> *Into your garth this day I did pursew;*
> *There saw I flowris that fresh were of hew;*
> > *Both white and red most lusty were to seene*

Devotion

And halesome herbis upon stalkis greene;
Yet leaf nor flowr find could I none of rew.

I doubt that Merche, with his cauld blastis keene,
Has slain this gentil herb, that I of mene;
Whose piteous death does to my heart such paine
That I would make to plant his root againe,—
So comforting his leavis unto me bene.

And along with the influx of Anglo-French words further
semantic changes were, of course, taking place in the more
important Old English words. If there are occasions when
a single word seems to throw more light on the workings
of men's minds than a whole volume of history or a whole
page of contemporary literature, the Middle English *love-
longing* is certainly one of them.

A new element had entered into human relationships, for
which perhaps the best name that can be found is 'tenderness'. And so—at any rate in the world of imagination—
children as well as women gradually became the objects of
a new solicitude. We do not find in all literature prior to
the Middle Ages quite that *pathetic* sense of childhood which
Chaucer has expressed so delicately in the story of Ugolino
of Pisa in his *Monk's Tale*:

> *But litel out of Pize stant[1] a tour*
> *In whiche tour in prisoun put was he,*
> *And with hym been his litel children three,*
> *The eldest scarsly fyf yeer was of age.*
> *Allas, Fortune! it was greet crueltee*
> *Swiche briddes[2] for to put in swiche a cage!*

[1] Stands.   [2] Birds.

Quotations are scarcely needed to intimate how such colourless words as *little*—here sentimentally repeated—*children*, and even *cruelty*, had gradually been laden with fresh emotional significance by the Roman Church's worship of the baby Jesus and its popular expression in carol and drama. We still have a few examples of these old Nativity Plays, from the individual scenes of which we take the word *pageant*, and about the same time that Chaucer wrote we know that the tailors of Coventry composed and sang the beautiful carol which begins:

> *Lully, lullay, thou little tiny Child,*
> *By by lully, lullay.*
> > *Herod the King*
> > *In his raging*
> *Charged he hath this day*
> > *His men of might*
> > *In his own sight*
> *All young children to slay. . . .*

Thus, when Tindale and Coverdale came to make their translations of the Bible in the sixteenth century, they found ready to their hand a vocabulary of feeling which had indeed been drawn in the first place from the austerities of the religious life, but which had in many cases acquired warmer and more human echoes by having been applied to secular uses. And just as lyrical devotion to the Virgin Mary and to the infant Jesus had helped to evolve a vocabulary which could express, and thus partly create, a sentiment of tenderness towards all women and young children, so we seem to feel the warmth of human affection, as it were, reflected back into religious emotion in such creations as Coverdale's *lovingkindness* and *tender mercy*, Tindale's *long-suffering*, *mercifulness*, *peacemaker*, and *beautiful* (for it was he who brought this word into general use), and in many of the majestically simple phrases of the Authorised Version.

In tracing the elements of modern consciousness through the history of words in this way, there is one mistake which it is especially important to avoid, and that is the mistake of over-simplification. For instance, just as it is true that the shade of feeling which we call 'tenderness' can be traced back to the literature of the Middle Ages, and that from there we can trace it farther back still, through the Mariolatry of the Roman Church to the opening chapters of the Luke Gospel, and so, maybe, to the old Egyptian Isis-worship and the philosophy of Plato, so it is also true that it can be understood more perfectly and felt more fully when we have thus unravelled it. But not to realize that with the appearance of a poetic tradition which can give rise to such a poem as 'I sing of a maiden' something quite new, something with no perceptible historical origin, enters into humanity, is to cultivate a deaf ear to literature, and to mistake quite as grievously both the method and the object of understanding history.

If medieval Europe is cut off from Greece and Rome by her imaginative conception of women, she is cut off even more completely by her abstention from slavery. Of this development, thus negatively stated, there are few, if any, signs in our language; but traces are by no means wanting of a certain deeper and more interior change which must have underlain the other two. Perhaps it can best be expressed as a new consciousness of the individual human soul. On the one hand the sense of its independent *being* and activity, of bottomless depths and soaring heights within it, to be explored in fear and trembling or with hope and joy—with *delight* and *mirth*, or with *agony, anguish, despair, repentance*—and on the other hand that feeling of its being an *inner* world, which has since developed so fully that this book, for example, has fallen naturally into two halves.

In this connection it is particularly interesting to note the appearance of *conscience* in the thirteenth century. In classical times the Latin 'conscientia' seems to have meant something more like 'consciousness' or 'knowledge'; it was generally qualified by some other word ('virtutum, vitiorum'—'consciousness of virtues, of vices,'...), and its termination, similar to that of *science, intelligence,* ... suggests that it was conceived of by the Romans more as a general, *abstract* quality, which one would partake of, but not actually possess—just as one has knowledge or happiness, but not 'a knowledge' or 'a happiness'. Used in ecclesiastical Latin and later in English, *conscience* seems to have grown more and more real, until at last it became that semi-personified and perfectly private mentor whom we are inclined to mean today when we speak of 'my *conscience*' or 'his *conscience*'.

The movement towards 'individualism', like many other phenomena of modern civilization, has long ago shifted its centre of gravity outside the walls of the Church. Once it was felt as the peculiar glory of the Christian religion. In the Dark Ages heresies which attempted to explain away the significant paradox of Christ's simultaneous divinity and humanity were hunted down with the utmost rigour, and it is probable that a vivid sense of the dignity of the individual human soul was at the bottom of a good many actions which now seem to us like the very stultification of such a conviction. This great inner world of consciousness, we may suppose, which each individual was now felt to control in some measure for himself, was a thing to fear as well as to respect. It gave to every single soul almost infinite potentialities, for evil as well as good; and even the wisest heads seem to have felt that civilization could only be held together as long as all these souls maintained a certain uniformity of pattern. Thus, while the influence of Christianity had ensured to all men—not merely to a small slave-owning class—a modicum of personal liberty, it deprived them in the same breath of that dearest of all possessions, freedom of thought. The grim meaning gradually acquired by the Latin word *Inquisition*, meaning an 'inquiry', still signifies to us the ruthless pains that were now taken, for the first time in the world's history, to pry into and endeavour to control that private thinking life of men which had suddenly acquired such a vast importance in their eyes. The still grimmer *auto-da-fé* began life as a Spanish phrase meaning simply an 'act of faith'.

It seems remarkable to us that, in spite of this active discouragement of independent thinking, the Dark and Middle Ages were, beyond dispute, the cradle of European philosophy. Perhaps this was because men did not yet feel the need for such independence. The leading quality of medieval thought was its receptiveness, and towards the end of its life it seems to have become almost conscious of this itself; for it is hardly possible to open a

volume of Chaucer without lighting on some half-respect-
ful, half-ironical reference to 'olde clerkes' or 'olde bokes'.
But the profound respect in which the written word had
been held throughout the Middle Ages survives in many
other curious ways as well. We still use the word *authority*
in its two separate meanings of 'a quotation from a book'
and 'the power of controlling'. Of these the first meaning
is the older, and from the twelfth to the sixteenth centuries
it may almost be said to have included the latter within it.
Again, our word *glamour*, a later form of *gramarye*, suggests
—or suggested, before it was debauched by Hollywood
and the popular press—an almost mystical reverence for the
'grammar' which—along with most of the other branches
of medieval learning—was derived entirely from the works
of Aristotle. The popularity and general use of *term*, which
began life as a subtle technicality of Aristotelian logic,
reminds us again of the universal study of that writer
in the Middle Ages, and *spice*—a corrupted form of
'species'—is but another indication of the way in which
the jargon of classical philosophy crept into their everyday
thought.

The change from Greek and Roman civilization to the
civilization of modern Europe is often represented as having been more abrupt than it really was. We have deduced
some of the intermediate stages in the alterations of feeling.
In the world of thought there are actual written documents
for our information, philosophical treatises and counter-
treatises, which, by revealing to us the very moment of
impact, enable us to trace more easily the reverberation of
thought from mind to mind. Not so long after the break up
of Rome, when the Empire was being partially reorganized

under Teutonic dynasties and the defunct Latin *Caesar*
rising again as the Germanic *Kaiser*, the great medieval
'Schools', of which the most famous was at Paris, began to
arise out of the traditions of monastic learning. Their
classical library apparently consisted of one Platonic dialogue and two or three works of Aristotle, all of them
translated; but the authority of these translations was absolute. At first Plato was considered the greater 'authority',
but from the beginning of the thirteenth century it seems to
have been accepted almost as a matter of course that the one
great object of all philosophy for all time was the harmon-
ization of Aristotelian logic and Catholic dogma. But
though the Aristotelian method (as they understood it) was
all in all, the actual Platonic system, with the help of Neoplatonism and the Mystics, lingered in sufficient strength to
divide medieval philosophy for several hundred years into
two rival camps. The one party, known as 'Realists', held
with Plato that 'ideas'—now usually called *universals*—had
existed before, and could exist quite apart from, things;
while the 'Nominalists' held that universals had no separate
or previous existence. But as time passed, many of the
Nominalists went farther still, maintaining that these universals did not exist at all, that they were mere intellectual
abstractions or classifications made by the human mind—in
fact 'ideas' in the sense in which, owing to them, we use the
word today. One of the reasons—perhaps the chief reason
—why so many Schoolmen carried Aristotle beyond himself in this way is a particularly interesting one.

Reference has already been made to the wave of Arabic
civilization which surged into Europe early in the Dark
Ages. It was a civilization in every sense of the word; for in

the ninth century learning had developed under the Caliphs of Baghdad to a degree unparalleled elsewhere in the world, and *rapprochements* between the two races and civilizations, which had already begun in the world of philosophy, were soon strengthened and increased by those great medieval experiments, the Crusades.[1] Now Arabic scholars were, if anything, more enthusiastic Aristotelians than the scholars of Europe. The curious word *arabesque,* and the fact that words like *algebra, cipher, zero,* and some others to be mentioned in the next chapter, are among the few Arabic words which reached our language before the fourteenth century, are both symptomatic of a certain peculiarity of the Arabic mind which we may perhaps call the tendency to abstraction. The Arab seems to have possessed something of that combination of materialism on the one hand and excessive intellectual abstraction on the other which we have already noticed in the later stages of Roman mythology. Just as he made Mohammedanism out of the Jewish sacred traditions, so he made Nominalism out of Greek philosophy. The influence upon Christian thought of great Arabic philosophers like Averroes and Avicenna is one of the most astonishing

---

[1] More direct products of the Crusades may be found in our language in the words *azure, cotton, orange, saffron, scarlet, sugar,* and *damask* (from the town of Damascus), all of which come to us either from Arabic or, through Arabic, from some Oriental language. *Miscreant* (misbeliever) was applied to the Mohammedans by the French Crusaders. *Assassin* (hashish-eaters) was used by the Christians to describe the secret murderers sent out by the Old Man of the Mountains against their leaders, because they used to intoxicate themselves with hashish before the interview. *Hazard*—originally a game played with dice—has been traced to Asart, the name of a castle in Palestine, during the siege of which it is said to have been invented; and *termagant* was first used in medieval romances as the name of one of the idols which the Saracens were supposed to worship.

chapters in its history. But it is not difficult to see how it occurred. The learning of the Middle Ages was founded entirely on translations, and this was an activity in which, as far as Aristotle's works were concerned, the Arabs had got in first. According to Renan, some of the current versions of Aristotle were 'Latin translations from a Hebrew translation of a Commentary of Averroes made on an Arabic translation of a Syriac translation of a Greek text'.

To the Popes and those who had the power and interest of the Church most at heart the problem appeared in quite a different light. It was a question of steering Christian dogma between the Scylla of pantheism and the Charybdis of materialism and its logical conclusion, scepticism. Thus, throughout the history of Scholasticism we have to do with a sort of triangle of intellectual forces: Realism and Nominalism fighting a five hundred years' war, and the Church, in its official capacity, anxiously endeavouring to hold the balance between them. One wonders whether the three parties to this ancient dispute may not have found symbolic expression in Tweedledum, Tweedledee, and the 'Monstrous Crow' of nursery legend. But it is no disparagement of the intellects of that day to say that to us the chief interest of their polemics lies in the many new and accurate instruments of thought with which they provided us. The common word *accident* is an excellent example. We use it every day without realizing that it was only imported from Latin by the indefatigable efforts of the Schoolmen to reconcile the doctrine of Realism with the Catholic dogma of Transubstantiation. The *accidents*, when they first came into the English language, meant that part of the sacred bread and wine which remained after the *substance* had been transmuted into the body and blood of Christ.

On the whole it is a safe rule to assume that those who speak most contemptuously of such thinkers as Thomas Aquinas and Duns Scotus are the nearest modern representatives of their own idea of what these Schoolmen were; that is to say, they are those whose imaginations are most completely imprisoned within the intellectual horizon of the passing age. Much fun has been made of medieval philosophy for discussing such matters as how many angels can stand on the point of a needle, and whether Christ could have performed His cosmic mission equally well if He had been incarnated as a pea instead of as a man. The growth of a rudimentary historical sense has, it is true, made it fashionable lately to take these ancient thinkers rather more seriously, but it is still rare to find a philosopher or a psychologist who fully comprehends that he is consuming the fruits of this long, agonizing struggle to state the exact relation between spirit and matter, every time he uses such key-words of thought as *absolute, actual, attribute, cause, concept, deduction, essence, existence, intellect, intelligence, intention, intuition, motive, potential, predicate, substance, tendency, transcend; abstract* and *concrete, entity* and *identity, matter* and *form, quality* and *quantity, objective* and *subjective, real* and *ideal, general, special* and *species, particular, individual,* and *universal.* 'Free will' is the translation of a Latin phrase first used by a Church Father, and 'argumentum ad hominem' is an example of a scholastic idiom which has remained untranslated. Many of these words, it is true, are in the first instance Latin translations of Greek terms introduced by pagan writers before the days of the Schoolmen; some, like *quality* and *species*, by Cicero himself, and others, like *accident*, *actual*, and *essence*, by later Latin writers such as Quintilian or Macrobius. But it must be remembered that, even in these cases, the words, as we use them today, are not *mere* translations. By their earnest and lengthy discussions the Schoolmen were all the time defining more strictly the meanings of these and of many other words already in use, and so adapting them to the European brain that in the thirteenth and fourteenth centuries it was an easy matter for the lawyers and for popular writers like Chaucer and Wyclif to stamp them with the authentic genius of the English language and turn them into current coin.[1] Nobody who understands the amount of pain and energy which go to the creation of new instruments of thought can feel anything but respect for the philosophy of the Middle Ages.

If the philosophy of the Middle Ages is based on the logic of Aristotle, their science can be traced rather to the Greek thought of pre-Aristotelian times. For authority it relied very largely on a single dialogue of Plato, to which may be added Latin translations of a small part of Hippocrates, and of his post-Christian successor and interpreter, Galen. But the way in which its terms have entered right into the heart of our language is proof enough that this medieval science arose, not merely from blind subservience to tradition, but also from an actual survival of the kind of feeling, the kind of outlook which, ages ago, had created the tradition. In

---

[1] In many cases, such as 'the *premises*', *predicament*, *nonentity*, . . . these austere old words have acquired colloquial meanings a long way removed from the exact philosophical thoughts which they were originally coined to express.

spite of that strong and growing sense of the individual soul, man was not yet felt, either physically or psychically, to be isolated from his surroundings in the way that he is today. Conversely his mind and soul were not felt to be imprisoned within, and dependent upon, his body. Intellectual classifications were accordingly less dry and clear, and science—that general speculative activity which a later age has split up into such categories as astronomy, physics, chemistry, physiology, psychology, . . .—was as yet almost an undivided whole. Common words like *ascendant, aspect, atmosphere, choleric, common sense, complexion, consider, cordial, disaster, disposition, distemper, ether, hearty, humour, humorous, indisposed, influence, jovial, lunatic, melancholy, mercurial, phlegmatic, predominant, sanguine, saturnine, spirited, temper, temperament,* with *heart, liver, spleen,* and *stomach* in their psychological sense, most of which retained their original and literal meanings down to the fourteenth century, give us more than a glimpse into the relations between body, soul, and cosmos, as they were felt by the medieval scientist.

Thus, the physical body was said to contain four *humours* (Latin 'humor', 'moisture')—*blood, phlegm, bile* or *choler,* and *black bile* (melancholy)—which last had its seat in the *hypochondria.* Not only diseases, or *distempers,* but qualities of character were intimately connected with the proper 'mixture' (Latin 'temperamentum') of these humours, just as modern medical theory sees a connection between the character and the glands. Thus, a man might be good *humoured* or bad *humoured*; he might have a good *temper* or a bad *temper*; and according to which *humour* predominated in his *temperament* or *complexion,* he was *choleric, melancholy, phlegmatic,* or *sanguine.* His character depended on other things as well; for the medieval scientist believed with Hippocrates that the arteries of the body were ducts through which there flowed, not blood, but three different kinds of *ether* (Greek 'aithēr', 'the upper air') or *spirits* (Latin 'spiritus', 'breath', 'life'), viz. the *animal*[1] (Latin 'anima', 'soul'), the *vital*, and the *natural*. But the stars and the planets were also living bodies; they were composed of that 'fifth essence' or *quintessence*, which was likewise latent in all terrestrial things, so that the character and the fate of men were determined by the *influences* (Latin 'influere', 'to flow in') which came from them. The Earth had its *atmosphere* (a kind of breath which it exhaled from itself); the Moon, which was regarded as a planet, had a special connection with *lunacy*, and according as the planet Jupiter, or Saturn, or Mercury was *predominant* or in the *ascendant* in the general *disposition* of stars at a man's birth, he would be *jovial*, *saturnine*, or *mercurial*. Finally, things or persons which were susceptible to the same *influences*, or which *influenced* each other in this occult way, were said to be in *sympathy* or *sympathetic*.

Test is an alchemist's word, coming from the Latin 'testa', an earthen pot in which the alchemist made his alloys. The same word was once used as a slang term for 'head', and in its French form, 'tête', still retains that meaning. The phrase *hermetically sealed* reminds us that alchemy, known as the 'hermetic art', was traced back by its exponents to the mysterious Hermes Trismegistus, who himself took his name from the Greek messenger-god Hermes. Other alchemists' words are *amalgam*, *alcohol*,

---

[1] Hence *animal spirits*. It is interesting to observe how this word, and the phrase, practically reversed their meanings in the seventeenth century.

alembic, alkali, elixir, and *tartar.* The last five, together with the word *alchemy* itself, all come to us from Arabic, and are evidence of the fact that the Arabs of the Dark Ages, besides being philosophers, were the fathers of modern chemistry. It was, indeed, they who first joined the study of chemistry to the practice of medicine, and thus initiated a science of drugs. Moreover, that old 'humoral' pathology which has shaped so many of our conceptions of human character—in so far as it was based on ancient authority and tradition—came from Hippocrates to Europe, for the most part not directly, but by way of Baghdad and Spain.

The more intimate and indispensable such conceptions are, the more effort does it require from the twentieth-century imagination to realize how they have grown up. It is so difficult, even when we are reading the old books themselves, to blot out from our consciousness the different meanings which have since gathered round the words. If, however, we can succeed in doing this, we cannot but be struck by the odd nature of the change which they have all undergone. When we reflect on the history of such notions as *humour, influence, melancholy, temper,* and the rest, it seems for the moment as though some invisible sorcerer had been conjuring them all inside ourselves—sucking them away from the planets, away from the outside world, away from our own warm flesh and blood, down into the shadowy realm of thoughts and feelings. There they still repose; astrology has changed to astronomy; alchemy to chemistry; today the cold stars glitter unapproachable overhead, and with a naïve detachment mind watches matter moving incomprehensibly in the void. At last, after four centuries, thought has shaken herself free.

VIII

EXPERIMENT

ZENITH · LAW · INVESTIGATE · CONCEIT · GENTLEMAN
LOVE · PROTESTANT

Philosophy, alchemy, and mathematics were not the only branches of learning in which the Arabs had excelled. The appearance in English of such words as *azimuth*, *nadir*, and *zenith* towards the end of the fourteenth century suggests among other things that the thinking of this Syrian race contributed in no small degree to the rise in Europe of the new astronomy. These three Arabic words (two of them for the first time in English) are to be found in Chaucer's *Treatise on the Astrolabe*, written in 1391 for the instruction of his little son, 'Lowis'; and this interesting document contains many other words also for which the *Oxford Dictionary* does not give any earlier quotation, such as *almanac*, *ecliptic*, *equinox*, *equator*, *horizon*, *latitude*, *longitude*, *meridian*, *minute* (meaning one-sixtieth of a degree), while *zodiac* was used by Gower a few years before.

Such words show us that the Europe of the Dark Ages had been experiencing once more what the ancient scientists had known. Its learned men had been marking down recurrences of natural phenomena and orientating them-

144

selves on the earth by dividing its face up into imaginary rings and segments. For such purposes they had found Latin and Greek terms ready to their hand, and the survival of the Greek *zodiac* reminds us that they had, moreover, adopted the ancient system of mapping out the heavens into twelve 'signs'. When, therefore, we find three Arabic words among these relics of classical wisdom, we need not be surprised to see that they express something which the ancients had, apparently, never felt the need of expressing —that is, an abstracted geometrical way of mapping out the visible heavens. These are conceived of as a vast sphere encircling the earth; the *zenith* and the *nadir* are its poles, while the *azimuths* are meridians of celestial longitude.

It is probable that, with the use of these words, there came for the first time into the consciousness of man the possibility of seeing himself purely as a solid object situated among solid objects. Of course, the Arab astronomer of the Dark and Middle Ages still saw the earth as the centre round which the universe revolved, and he would no more have dreamed of doubting the 'astral' quality of the planets than the schoolmaster of today who instructs his pupils to write down 'Let $x=20$ oranges' doubts whether oranges have any taste. Nevertheless we may feel pretty sure that those minds which were apparently the first to think of cutting up the sky without reference to the constellations, and which could, moreover, develop so fully the great and novel system of abstraction which they called *algebra*, did their part in bringing about that extraordinary revolution in astronomical thought which is associated with the name of Copernicus. It is true that the astronomy of Plato's time had been intimately connected with arithmetic and geometry; but Plato's 'number' and his geometry do not appear to have been quite the abstract sciences which these things are today. What we call their 'laws' seem to have been felt, not as intellectual deductions, but rather as real activities of soul—that human soul which, as we saw, the philosopher could not yet feel to be wholly separate from a larger world Soul, or planetary Soul. The Zodiacal signs, for instance, had been as much, if not more, classifications of this Soul as they had been sections of space. The word comes from the Greek 'zōdion', a little animal, and not only was every sign distinguished by a constellation, of which the majority were associated with some beast, but human character and human destiny were believed to be bound up inextricably with the position of the sun and the planets among these signs.

If, therefore, there is any truth in the belief of the old Greek philosophers and of some modern historians that the study of mathematics has its origin in the observed movements of the stars, the progress is of the same nature as that which we noticed at the end of the last chapter. Is it too fanciful to picture to ourselves how, drawn into the minds of a few men, the relative positions and movements of the stars gradually developed a more and more independent life there until, with the rise in Europe first of trigonometry and then of algebra, they detached themselves from the outside world altogether? And then by a few great men like Copernicus, Kepler, Galileo, Newton, these abstract mathematics were re-fitted to the stars which had given them birth, and the result was that cosmogony of infinite spaces and a tiny earth in which our imaginations roam today? When the Aryan imagination had at last succeeded in so detaching its 'ideas' about the phenomena of the universe that these could be 'played with', as mathematicians say, in the form of an equation, then, no doubt, it was a fairly easy matter to turn them inside out.

The alterations wrought in the meanings of many of our common words by this revolution of physical outlook are not difficult to perceive and yet not easy to realize. As the discoveries of Kepler and Galileo slowly filtered through to the popular consciousness, first of all simple words like *atmosphere, down, earth, planet, sky, space, sphere, star, up,* . . . underwent a profound yet subtle semantic change. And then, in the eighteenth century, as Newton's discoveries became more widely known, further alterations took place. *Weight*,[1] for instance, acquired a new significance, differing from *mass*, which also changed, having formerly meant simply a lump of matter.[2] *Gravity*,[3] (from the Latin 'gravitas' 'heaviness') took on its great new meaning, and the new words *gravitation* and *gravitate* were formed, the latter being soon adapted to metaphorical uses. If we cared to examine them closely enough, we should probably find that from this point a certain change of meaning gradually spread over all words containing the notion of attraction, or ideas closely related to it. The twin phenomena of gravi-

[1] 'Heaviness or weight is not here considered, as being such a naturall *quality*, whereby condensed bodies do of themselves *tend downwards*; but rather as being an affection whereby they may be measured. And in this sense Aristotle himself referres it amongst the other *species* of *quantity*, as having the same proper essence, which is to be compounded of integrall parts. So a pound doth consist of ounces. . . .' (Bishop Wilkins: *Mathematicall Magick*, 1648.)

[2] Latin 'massa' (dough); from Greek 'massein' (to knead).

[3] 'With this kinde of Ballance, it is usuall . . . to measure sundry different gravities.' (*Mathematicall Magick.*)

tation and magnetism, contemplated by most of us at an early age, and impalpably present in the meanings of so many of the words we hear spoken around us, make the conception of one lifeless body acting on another from a distance seem easy and familiar.[1] But the very word *attraction* (from the Latin 'ad-trahere', 'to draw' or 'drag towards') may well serve to remind us that until the discovery of gravitation this conception must have been practically beyond the range of human intellection. There was formerly no half-way house in the imagination between actual dragging or pushing and forces emanating from a living being, such as love or hate, human or divine, or those 'influences' of the stars which have already been mentioned.

A good illustration of this fact—and one which takes us back again to the seventeenth century—is the word *law*. The Latin 'lex' was first applied to natural phenomena by Bacon. Later in the century *law* was used in the same sense, but it did not then mean quite what it does today. The 'laws of Nature' were conceived of by those who first

---

[1] To the ordinary, untrained imagination. Philosophers and scientists, however, have continued to boggle at this notion of action at a distance. Thus Leibnitz, shortly after Newton published his discovery: ''Tis also a supernatural thing that bodies should *attract* one another at a distance without any intermediate means.' And Huxley in 1886, on the terms *atom* and *force*: 'As real entities, having an objective existence, an indivisible particle which nevertheless occupies space is surely inconceivable; And with respect to the operation of that atom, where it is not, by the aid of a "force" resident in nothingness, I am as little able to imagine it as I fancy anyone else is.' Hence the invention of a hypothetical *ether*, in order that space might be supposed filled with a continuum of infinitely attenuated matter (p.165). In the world of scientific theory the question of action at a distance is still a fairly appetizing bone of contention.

spoke of them as present commands of God. It is noticeable that we still speak of Nature 'obeying' these laws, though we really think of them now rather as abstract principles—logical deductions of our own which we have arrived at by observation and experiment.

Some account of Francis Bacon's general influence, as a writer, on our language has already been given in Chapter IV. His influence on thought was far greater, for he was in some sense the moving spirit of that intellectual revolution which began to sweep over Europe in the sixteenth century. It was a revolution comparable in many ways to the change inaugurated by Aristotle twenty centuries earlier, and there is accordingly much in Bacon's work that reminds us of the Greek philosopher. To begin with, he was thoroughly dissatisfied with the whole *method* of thought as he found it in his day, and, like Aristotle, he strove first of all to effect a reformation in this. Aristotle had written the *Organum*—that is to say, the 'Instrument' (of Thought) —and Bacon intended his *Novum Organum* to go one step farther. He proclaimed himself satisfied with Aristotle's legacy—the prevailing logical system of syllogism and deduction—as far as it went. Given the 'premises', it was the correct line of further discovery. What he questioned was the Scholastic premises themselves, and he propounded accordingly a new and surer method of establishing fresh ones. It is known as the 'inductive method'. This is not the place to expound Bacon's logical system, and it will suffice that it was based on an extensive and, above all, a systematic observation of Nature herself. Aristotle had indeed (though the Schoolmen had nearly forgotten it) pointed the way to such an observation, but it was left for Bacon to try and

construct a prejudice-proof system of arranging and classi-
fying the results. These *instances*, as they were called, were,
on the one hand, to be manufactured by means of *experiment*, and on the other to be arranged and weeded out
according to their significance. The word *crucial* comes to
us from Bacon's Latin phrase 'instantia crucis'—the *crucial
instance*—which, like a sign-post, decided between two
rival hypotheses by proving one and disproving the other;
and it may be said that he endeavoured, but failed, to alter
the meaning of *axiom* itself from 'a self-evident proposition'
to 'a proposition established by the method of experimental induction'.

Once more men turned the light of their curiosity upon
the stubborn phenomena of the outside world, and as it was
Aristotle's works in which we first found the Greek *anatomy*, 'cutting up', so it is Bacon who first uses *dissection*
(from the Latin for the same thing) in its modern technical
meaning. After an interval of about 1,500 years, the weighing, measuring, examining, and cutting up had now begun
again, and they have gone on ever since. How far Francis
Bacon was responsible for the form subsequently taken by
scientific thought will probably remain a matter of dispute.
His views on ecclesiastical authority, on Scholastic philosophy, on Aristotle, on the Alchemists, certainly suggest
that he possessed what the nineteenth century has called the
'scientific attitude' to an extent which distinguishes him
startlingly from any previous or contemporary writer;
acid, *hydraulic*, and *suction* are among the words first found
in his pages; but, above all, his consciousness of greater
changes afoot is manifested linguistically in such things as
his use of the words *progressive* and *retrograde* in an historical

sense unknown, as we shall see, to the majority of thinkers until the middle of the eighteenth century, or his equally innovating distinction between *ancient* and *modern*. A marked increase over the second quarter of the seventeenth century in the number of words expressing the notion of doubt, such as *dubious* (used of opinions), *dubiousness, dubitable, sceptic, sceptical, sceptically, scepticism, scepticity, scepticize,* compares with an increase of only one or two during the fifteenth and sixteenth centuries. And at about the same time the words *curious, curiosity,* and *inquisitive* seem to have lost the air of pious disapproval which they had previously carried with them when used to express the love of inquiry. How much of this is due to novel combinations, such as 'a natural *curiosity* and *inquisitive* appetite', which we find in Bacon's *Advancement of Learning*? We cannot say. There are symptoms of the coming metamorphosis already, before his time, in the appearance in English of the sixteenth century of such significant new terms as *analyse, distinguish, investigate,* together with the semantic change of *observe* from 'to obey a rule', or 'to inspect auguries' into its modern meaning, and similar changes in the case of *experiment* and *experimental*. It is impossible to prove these things. As with Aristotle, so with Bacon, it is impossible to say whether his own intellectual volume displaced the great wave or whether he merely rose upon its early crest.

There are other influences, too, that must be taken into account. *Discovery* (it was a new word) was in the very air of sixteenth-century England. From the West came tidings of a new world; from the East news yet more marvellous of an old one; and the rebirth of Science was, in its infancy, but a single aspect of that larger Renaissance which played such an important part in moulding the subsequent life and outlook of Europe. Italy had felt the shock first, and we have a special group of words in our language to remind us of the visual arts in which the new impulse drove her to excel. *Cameo, cupola, fresco,* and *model* all reached us in the sixteenth century from or through the Italian, and the next saw the arrival of *attitude, bust, chiaroscuro, dado, dome, filigree, intaglio, mezzotinto,* and *pastel.* If these are of a somewhat technical nature, words like *antic, canto, capriole, galligaskins, sonnet,* and *stanza* build a bridge in the imagination from Renaissance Italy to Tudor England, and *ducat, incarnadine,* and *madonna* are three Italian words with pleasant Shakespearian associations. They remind us, too, that by the time the Renaissance reached England it was already in full swing. No wonder the literary world was swept off its feet. First-hand acquaintance with the works of Classical writers gradually substituted an affectionate, an almost passionate, familiarity for that religious awe with which the Middle Ages had honoured their garbled translations. One of the first results—an immediate and violent intellectual revolt against the Schoolmen and all things connected with them—is faithfully preserved to us in the unenviable immortality achieved about this time by the luckless Duns Scotus, whose patronymic has given us *dunce.* The history of the word *conceit,* which in Chaucer merely meant 'anything conceived', tells its tale of the wild, undiscriminating rush after elegance of thought and diction. By Shakespeare's time the tasteless habit of piling fanciful conceit upon conceit had already become a thing to parody, the merest affectation of wit, and so the word lives today chiefly as a synonym for personal vanity, the language having been obliged by its degradation to re-borrow the Latin original 'conceptus' in the more exact form of *concept*.

It can readily be imagined that the restless activity which these little symptoms betoken had a remarkable effect in altering, developing, and indeed modernizing, the English vocabulary. The genius of the language sprouted and burgeoned in the genial warmth of Elizabethan and Jacobean fancy, and—most effective of all—it passed through the fire of Shakespeare's imagination. There is an unobtrusiveness about Shakespeare's enormous influence on his native tongue which sometimes recalls the records of his private life. This is no doubt partly due to the very popularity of his plays, which has preserved the direct influence in every age. Where the word which he employs is a new one, it has usually become so common in the course of years that we find it hard to conceive of the time when it was not. Where it is a meaning or a shade of meaning which he has added, as likely as not that very shade was the one most familiar to our own childhood before we had ever read a line of his poetry. Phrases and whole lines from the plays and sonnets are as much a part of the English vocabulary as individual words. Such are *pitched battle, play on words, give him his due, well on your way, too much of a good thing, to the manner born, the glass of fashion, snapper-up of unconsidered trifles, more honoured in the breach than the observance,* . . . The influence of such a mind on the language in which it expresses itself can only be compared to the effect of high temperatures on solid matter. As imagination bodies forth the forms of things unknown, each molecule of suggestiveness contained in each word gains a mysterious freedom from its neighbours; the old images move to and fro distinctly in the listener's fancy, and when the sound has died away, not merely the shape, but what seemed to be the very substance of the word has been readjusted.

Examples are found readily enough with the help of a volume of Shakespeare and the *Oxford Dictionary*. As to new words themselves, it has been said that there are more in Shakespeare's plays than in all the rest of the English poets put together. *Advantageous, amazement, critic* and *critical, dishearten, dwindle, generous, invulnerable, majestic, obscene, pedant, pious, radiance, reliance,* and *sanctimonious* are a few examples, but it is still more interesting to trace the subtler part of his influence. As an instance of what we may call his literary alertness let us take the word *propagate*. It is not found in English before 1570, and is thus a new word in Shakespeare's time. Yet he handles it four times, now literally, now figuratively, with as much ease and grace as if it had been one of the oldest words in the language. Listen to Romeo:

> *Griefs of mine own lie heavy in my breast,*
> *Which thou wilt propagate, to have it prest*
> *With more of thine.*

Again, the figurative—that is to say, the only modern use of *influence*—is first quoted from his works, and we can watch him gradually taking the meaning of the word *sphere* through its historical developments of planetary 'sphere', high social rank, any sort of category. A certain curious intransitive use of the verb *take*, as when a doctor says 'the vaccination *took* very well', can also be traced back to Shakespeare, and a few more of the innumerable new uses of words which appear to have begun from him are *sequence* and *creed*, with purely secular meanings; *real*, in its ordinary modern sense of 'actual'; *magic, magical*, and *charm*,[1] used figuratively; *apology* as the personal and verbal expression of compunction; *positive* in its psychological sense; *function*, used biologically; *fashion* and *fashionable* with their modern meanings; and *action*, meaning a battle. The fact that the first examples of these new uses quoted in the *Oxford Dictionary* are taken from Shakespeare cannot, of course, be taken as absolute proof that he introduced them. But there are so many of them, and the *Dictionary* is so thorough, that there can be little doubt of his being the first in many cases and among the first in every case.

Shakespeare's influence on the personal relations between the sexes, as they have developed in subsequent periods of English history, is a matter for the literary and social historian; but it is interesting to reflect how the meanings of that group of Norman French words mentioned in the last chapter, and of others which were slowly drawn into their circle, must have expanded under the warm breath of his vivacious and human heroines. The ideal atmosphere of gracious tenderness which was the contribution to humanity of the Middle Ages was to some extent realized by the Elizabethans. The women towards whom it was directed became less and less mere ecclesiastical or poetical symbols, existing only in the imagination of the lover, and more and more creatures of real flesh and blood. Once again it is a

---

[1] The transition of meaning is beautifully visible in the following passage from *The Merry Wives of Windsor*:

Mistress Quickly: 'I never knew a woman so dote upon a man: surely, I think you have charms, la; yes, in truth.'

Falstaff: 'Not I, I assure thee: setting the attraction of my good parts aside, I have no other charms.'

case of a later age striving to live out what an earlier age—
or its few best minds—have dreamed. Thus, the Blessed
Virgin is partly supplanted in men's hearts by the virgin
Queen; the charming figure of Sidney—personified gentle-
ness and chivalry—actually passes across the stage of history; the peculiarly English word *gentleman* appears. And
we can hardly help holding Shakespeare partly responsible
for what is going forward when we find him writing 'the
devout religion of mine eye' and making Richard III im-
plore Anne to 'let the soul forth that adoreth thee'—where
the words *religion* and *adore* are both applied to humanity
for the first time, as far as we know, in English literature.

Moreover, the new access to the Classics added to all this
the direct influence of the Platonic philosophy which now
played, through Spenser and his circle, upon the thought
and feeling of the Elizabethan age. A careful reading of
Spenser's four hymns to *Love, Beauty, Heavenly Love,* and
Heavenly Beauty will throw much light on the subsequent
semantic history of the title words and of many others. We
find in them the Platonic antithesis between the Eternal and
its for-ever-changing outward garment:

> *For that same goodly hew of white and red,*
> *With which the cheekes are sprinckled, shall decay,*
> *And those sweete rosy leaves so fairely spread*
> *Upon the lips, shall fade and fall away*
> *To that they were, even to corrupted clay.*
> *That golden wyre, those sparckling stars so bright*
> *Shall turne to dust, and loose their goodly light.*
>
> *But that faire lampe, from whose celestial ray*
> *That light proceedes, which kindleth lovers' fire,*

Shall never be extinguisht nor decay,
But when the vitall spirits doe expyre,
Unto her native planet shall retyre,
For it is heavenly borne and can not die,
Being a parcell of the purest skie.

and the conception of contemplation rising, through love, from the one to the other, as in

For love is Lord of truth and loialtie,
Lifting himselfe out of the lowly dust,
On golden plumes up to the purest skie. . . .

or:

But they which love indeede, look otherwise,
With pure regard and spotless true intent,
Drawing out of the object of their eyes
A more refyned forme, which they present
Unto their minde. . . .

until finally, in the *Hymne of Heavenly Beauty*, Spenser reveals the source of his faith:

Faire is the heaven, where happy soules have place,
In full enjoyment of felicitie. . . .

More faire is that where those Idees *on hie,*
Enraunged be, which Plato *so admyred,*
And pure Intelligences *from God inspyred.*

When we recall the great influence which Spenser's poetry has exerted on English poets who have lived and written since his day, we can clearly see how the two kinds of Platonism—a direct Platonism, and a Platonism long ago transmuted and worked right down into the emotions of

common people by the passionate Christianity of the Dark
and Middle Ages—combined to beget the infinite suggestiveness which is now contained in such words as *love* and
beauty. Let us remember, then, that every time we abuse
these terms, or use them too lightly, we are draining them
of their power; every time a society journalist or a film
producer exploits this vast suggestiveness to tickle a vanity
or dignify a lust, he is squandering a great pile of spiritual
capital which has been laid up by centuries of weary
effort.

The fact that a great deal of what had formerly been
religious emotion was being secularized in this way does
not, however, mean that the Church had ceased to play an
all-important part in the life of the people. The Reformation seems, with its insistence on the *inwardness* of all true
grace, to have been but another manifestation of that steady
shifting inwards of the centre of gravity of human consciousness which we have already observed in the scientific
outlook. That shift is, in a larger sense, the story told by the
whole history of the Aryan languages. Thus *religion* itself,
which had formerly been used only of external observances
or of monastic orders, took on at about this time its modern, subjective meaning. Now it was that *piety*, differen-
tiating itself from *pity*, began to acquire its present sense.
Godly, *godliness*, and *godless* are first found in Tindale's
writings, and *evangelical* and *sincere* are words which have
been noted by a modern writer as being new at this time
and very popular among the Protestants. The great word
Protestant itself was applied formerly to the German princes
who had dissented from the decision of the Diet of Spires
in 1529, and together with *Reformation* it now acquired its

new and special meaning, while the old words, *dissent* and *disagree*, were transferred at about the same time from material objects to matters of opinion.

Another little group of words which appeared in the language at about this time is interesting in its suggestion that human emotions, like the forces of Nature, are usually accompanied by their equal and opposite reactions. The well-known phrases, *odium theologicum* and *odium philosophicum*, survive to remind us of a new kind of bitterness and hatred which had slowly been arising in men's hearts, and which were also, it would seem, the gifts of Christianity and the Dark Ages. Very soon after the Reformation we find alongside the syllables of tenderness and devotion a very pretty little vocabulary of abuse. *Bigoted, faction, factious, malignant, monkish, papistical, pernicious, popery* are among the products of the struggle between Catholic and Protestant; and the terms *Roman, Romanist*, and *Romish* soon acquired such a vituperative sense that it became necessary to evolve *Roman Catholic* in order to describe the adherents of that faith without giving offence to them. The later internecine struggles among the Protestants themselves gave us *Puritan, precise, libertine*—reminiscent of a time when 'liberty' of thought was assumed as a matter of course to include licence of behaviour—*credulous, superstitious, selfish, selfishness*, and the awful Calvinistic word *reprobate*. It was towards the end of the Puritan ascendancy that *atone* and *atonement* (*at-one-ment*) acquired their present strong suggestion of legal expiation, and it may not be without significance that the odious epithet *vindictive* was then for the first time applied approvingly to the activities of the Almighty Himself.

Experiment

As the language grows older, when all the principal tributaries have met at last in the main stream, it begins, unfortunately, to tell a less and less coherent tale of the people who speak it. The few large groups of new words and meanings which we have hitherto been tracing give way to a much greater number of small groups—or even of single words—for the vocabulary is now so capacious that important new movements of thought are likely to find the old terms adaptable to their use with very slight semantic alterations, or perhaps with the formal addition of an -*arian*, an -*ism*, or an -*ology*. These become accordingly harder to trace, and a book of these dimensions is obliged to select a word here and a word there in almost arbitrary fashion. It must be remembered, then, in this and the succeeding chapters that only a few of the tendencies and changes at work have been picked out for inspection, though it is probable that a study of words, which should be at the same time subtle and comprehensive enough, would throw some light on them all.

IX

PERSONALITY AND REASON

PRIG · PRESSURE · PERIOD · CONSCIOUSNESS · CHARACTER
AMUSING · SENTIMENTAL · ARRANGE · PERSONIFY

When Charles II returned from France to an England which had long been growing more and more sullen under the reproving glances of a middle-aged Puritanism, the suppressed thoughts and feelings of fashionable English society evidently lost no time in rising to the surface. The appearance in the seventeenth century of new expressions such as to *banter*, to *burlesque*, to *ridicule*, to *prim*, *travesty*, *badinage*, and, above all, *prig*, helps to fill in for the imagination the deep gulf between the *Pilgrim's Progress* and the *Country Wife*. Even to those totally unacquainted with the literature of the period this little archipelago of words might betray with unmistakable solidity the moral geography of the submerged region. For it marks a cycle of events which has been repeated over and over again in the history of humanity, in its families, its societies, its nations. Certain moral qualities gain respect for themselves; the respect brings with it material benefits; weaker brethren affect the moral qualities in order to acquire the material benefits; hypocrisy is detected; all morality is treated as hypocrisy. The trite little cycle spins like a whirligig round and round the social history of the world, but this is a good place to lay a finger on it, for it is a process in which the question of the meanings of words takes a particularly active part. It is, in fact, one of the few occasions upon which ordinary men, neither scientists nor poets, will deliberately attempt to alter the meanings of the words they must use. 'Morality', said the late Sir Walter Raleigh, 'colours all language and lends to it the most delicate of its powers of distinction'; and so, when any significant change takes place in the moral standards of a community, it is immediately reflected in a general shifting of the meanings of common words.

One of the earliest recorded examples of such a shift is analysed with sharp penetration by Thucydides in his account of the demoralization of the Greek States during the Peloponnesian War:

'Proper shame (he says) is now termed sheer stupidity: shamelessness, on the other hand, is called manliness: voluptuousness passes for good tone: haughtiness for good education: lawlessness for freedom: honourable dealing is dubbed hypocrisy, and dishonesty, good fortune.

Similar, but less conspicuous and rapid, alterations of mood must have been at work when *silly* lost its old meaning of 'blessed'; when *demure* changed from 'grave' or 'sober' to 'affectedly modest'; and when the kindly *officious* acquired its modern sense of bustling interference. Trench regards it as a tribute to the Roman character that theirs is the only civilized language in which the word for 'simple' never acquired a contemptuous signification alongside of its ordinary one. And at the opposite pole from Thucydides we have another Aryan historian, Mr. G. K. Chesterton, good-humouredly suggesting what might be called a semantic method of slipping off a Semitic incubus:

'As for sin, let us call it folly and have done with it, for until we call it folly we never shall have done with it. The conception of sin flatters us grossly. There is something grandiose in it that cannot but appeal to the child in every man. That we infinitesimal creatures, scrambling like ants over the face of this minor planet in pursuit of our personal aims—that we have it in our power to affront the majesty of the universe is a most preposterous, delightful fancy . . .'

It may be remarked in passing that there is no surer or more illuminating way of reading a man's character, and perhaps a little of his past history, than by observing the contexts in which he prefers to use certain words. Each of us would no doubt choose his own list of test words—and the lists themselves, if we were foolish enough to reveal them, would probably present a fairly accurate diagram of our own leading propensities. Fortunately the subject is too long to elaborate.

Ogle is another new word which appeared soon after the Restoration; and at the same time *intrigue*, which had come into the language earlier in the century in the general sense of 'intricacy', was seized upon to express an illicit love-affair. The steady growth of 'polite' society during the seventeenth and eighteenth centuries is also—curiously enough—indicated by the gradual appearance of *bearish, countrified, fatuous, flippant, gawky, mawkish, prude,* and other such terms. *Hoyden* was first used of a girl by Wycherley in 1676.

But outside the limelit circle this period was one of rapid intellectual development. That the novel interest in the external world, typified in the sixteenth century by such new words as *analyse, distinguish, investigate*,[1] expanded continuously during the next hundred years is suggested by the addition to our vocabulary of *inspect, remark* and *scrutinize*, together with the modern meanings of *perception* and *scrutiny*, which had meant up till then respectively 'the collection of rents' and 'the taking of a vote'. We also find a group of new words to describe the inherent conditions and qualities of external objects, such as *acid, astringency, cohesion, elasticity, equilibrium, fluid* (as a noun), *intensity, polarity, pressure, spontaneous, static, temperature, tendency, tension, volatile*, besides the physical and impersonal meanings of *energy* and *force*. The old verb to *discover*, which originally signified simply to 'uncover' or 'reveal',[2] was used attributively in the sixteenth century of travellers 'discovering' foreign lands and customs. Shortly after the Restoration the new metaphor, so it would seem, was itself applied metaphorically to the results of a chemical experiment, and in this way the ordinary modern meaning arose. The creation of the new word *gas* by the Dutch chemist van Helmont marks a definite epoch in the evolution of the scientific outlook. He used it, however, to describe an occult principle—a sort of ultra-rarefied water—which he supposed to be contained in all matter. It was not until the last quarter of the eighteenth century that the word acquired its modern meaning of 'matter in the condition of an aeri-

[1] See p. 151.

[2] A meaning which it still retains in stage directions—e.g. 'The curtain rises, *discovering* N—— seated in an arm-chair'.

form fluid', at which time the word *gaseous* also appeared. *Ether* (Greek 'aithēr', 'the *upper* air' above the clouds), which had been practically a synonym for the Aristotelian *quintessence*,[1] was now adopted to express the mechanical substitute for that spiritual medium, required by modern science in order to explain the phenomenon of action at a distance. These are among the first attempts which were made to describe the outer world objectively—from its own point of view instead of from the point of view of divinity or of human souls; it is interesting, therefore, to reflect that the success achieved is really only a relative one, as all the words mentioned, with the possible exception of *gas*,[2] are in the first place metaphors drawn from human activities such as those of 'cutting', 'stretching', and 'pulling'.

In about the year 1660 the spirit of curious inquiry which was abroad prompted the foundation of the Royal Society, for the purpose, as its title announced, of 'Improving Natural Knowledge', and it is notable that the word *improve* should have been employed. Originating, as we saw, in Lawyer's French, it had been used up to about 1620 to denote merely 'the enclosure and cultivation of waste land'. So that when we find its old meaning butchered to make a striking metaphor, it is reasonable to assume that some new idea or feeling had come to the front, to which men were struggling to give the outward expression that is life, that their outlook had changed somewhat, and that

[1] See p. 142.

[2] Even gas, though it is an arbitrary creation, was intended by van Helmont to resemble *chaos*, a Greek word which is derived from a verb 'chaskein', meaning to 'yawn' or 'gape'.

they were groping for a means of readjusting their cosmos accordingly.

We have attempted so far to trace the evolution of Western outlook from the earliest days of Greece down to the Revival of Learning in England. It must not be forgotten that this process is hitherto an unconscious one. Up to the seventeenth century the outlook of the European mind upon the world, fluid as it has always been, has yet always felt itself to be at rest, just as men have hitherto believed that the earth on which they trod was a solid and motionless body. The first appearance of a distinction between *ancient* and *modern*, and of the word *progressive*, in Bacon's *Essays* has already been noted, and we find that *progress* itself had only begun to emerge a few years before from its relatively parochial meaning of 'royal journey' or, as we still say, 'progress'. To the seventeenth century, as Mr. Pearsall Smith has pointed out, we owe the words *antiquated, century, decade, epoch, Gothic, out-of-date, primeval,* and we may add to these *contemporary, contemporaneous, synchronize, synchronous,* and a queer jungle-growth of words with similar meanings which sprang up about the middle of the seventeenth century and has since vanished: *contemporal, co-temporary, contemporize, isochronal, synchronal, synchronical, synchronism, synchronistic.* A curious feature about these latter words is the number of them which first appeared in theological writings, the mystic philosopher, Henry More, being alone responsible for three. They seem to have arisen chiefly from an interest in comparing the dates of different events recorded in Scripture, and they may thus be placed beside the epithet *primitive*, applied by the Reformers to the early Church, which Mr. Pearsall

Smith has pointed to as 'probably the first word in which our modern historical sense finds expression'.

When we try combing the dictionaries—Greek, Latin, English, and others—for words expressing a sense of the 'march of history', or indeed of a past or future differing at all essentially from the present, we are forced to the conclusion that this kind of outlook on time is a surprisingly recent growth. We saw how the Greek 'historia' could mean practically any kind of knowledge; in the same way, when 'periodos' (literally 'way round') was used of time, it meant a cycle, one of a recurring series; it was not till the eighteenth century that a *period* of history acquired its modern sense of an indefinite portion cut from a continuous process. Labels like *Middle Ages, Renaissance, . . .* are none of them earlier than the eighteenth century, which also saw the new expressions *develop* and *development*, and the fact that the significant words *anachronism,*[1] *evolution,*[1] and *prehistoric*, with the new perspectives they denote, only appeared during the nineteenth century may make us doubtful whether the mists of time have even yet fallen wholly from our eyes.

In order to enter sympathetically into the outlook of an educated medieval gentleman, we have to perform the difficult feat of undressing, as it were, our own outlook by divesting it of all those seemingly innate ideas of progress and evolution, of a movement of some sort going on everywhere around us, which make our cosmos what it is. This is more difficult even than it sounds, because so many of these thoughts and feelings have become subconscious. We have imbibed them with our vocabulary and cannot without

[1] Except in old, particular senses, which they have now lost.

much labour and research disentangle the part that is due to them from the rest of our consciousness. Let us try, for a moment, to realize with our imaginations as well as with our intellects the world in which our fathers dwelt—a world created abruptly at a fixed moment in time, and awaiting a destruction equally abrupt, its inhabitants for ever to be the same, and for ever struggling, not to *progress* or to *evolve* into something different, but rather to become once more exactly like the first man and woman. Where we speak of *progress* and *evolution*, the Middle Ages could speak only of *regeneration* and *amendment*. Their evolution was like Alice's race with the Red Queen. It took all their energies to keep still; and even in this they had very little hope of succeeding, for they believed that the world was getting steadily worse.

But perhaps their total lack of historical imagination is brought home to us most forcibly by the prevalent belief that—apart from the Chosen People—all the inhabitants of the pre-Christian world were doomed to eternal exclusion from paradise. When we recollect that for some time the doctors of medieval universities were obliged to swear upon oath that they would teach nothing contrary to the doctrines of a Greek philosopher who must already have been in this situation for three hundred years at the birth of the Redeemer, and when we further reflect that it was the acute brains of these very doctors which were engaged in building up our present thinking apparatus, we may well feel inclined to give up as hopeless the task of sympathetically recreating the medieval cosmos in our imaginations— unless we realize, as indeed the history of meanings clearly shows, that it is not merely ideas and theories and feelings which have changed, but the very method of forming ideas and of combining them, the very channels, apparently eternal, by which one thought or feeling is connected with another. Possibly the Middle Ages would have been equally bewildered at the facility with which twentieth-century minds are brought to believe that, intellectually, humanity languished for countless generations in the most childish errors on all sorts of crucial subjects, until it was redeemed by some simple scientific dictum of the last century.

There is another difference between the past and the present which it is hard for us to realize; and perhaps this is the hardest of all. For with the seventeenth century we reach the point at which we must at last try to pick up and inspect that discarded garment of the human soul, intimate and close-fitting as it was, into which this book has been trying from the fifth chapter onwards to induce the reader to re-insert his modern limbs. The consciousness of 'myself' and the distinction between 'my-self' and all other selves, the antithesis between 'myself', the observer, and the external world, the observed, is such an obvious and early fact of experience to every one of us, such a fundamental starting-point of our life as conscious beings, that it really requires a sort of training of the imagination to be able to conceive of any different kind of consciousness. Yet we can see from the history of our words that this form of experience, so far from being eternal, is quite a recent achievement of the human spirit. It was absent from the old mythological outlook; absent, in its fullness, from Plato and the Greek philosophers; and, though it was beginning to light up in the Middle Ages, as we see in the development of Scholastic words like *individual* and *person*, yet the medieval soul was still felt to be joined by all sorts of occult ties both to the physical body and to the world. Self-consciousness, as we know it, seems to have first dawned faintly on Europe at about the time of the Reformation, and it was not till the seventeenth century that the new light really began to spread and brighten. One of the surest signs that an idea or feeling is coming to the surface of consciousness—surer than the appearance of one or two new words—is the tendency of an old one to form compounds and derivatives. After the Reformation we notice growing up in our language a whole crop of words hyphened with *self*; such are *self-conceit, self-liking, self-love,* and others at the end of the sixteenth century, and *self-confidence, self-command, self-contempt, self-esteem, self-knowledge, self-pity,* . . . in the next.

From a full list of such words as the above the historical student of words and their meanings could almost predict, apart from any other source of knowledge, the appearance at about this time of some philosopher who should do intellectually to the cosmos what Copernicus and Kepler had already done astronomically—that is, turn it inside out. And in Descartes, with his doctrine of 'Cogito, ergo sum', we do, in fact, find just such a philosopher. His influence was immense. Practically all philosophy since his day has worked outwards from the thinking self rather than inwards from the cosmos to the soul. In England, not long afterwards, we find the brand-new expressions, 'the *ego*' and *egoism,* coming into the language from French philosophy, while the English thinker, Locke, adopts the new (1632) word *consciousness,* defining it as 'perception of what passes in a man's own mind', and at the same time impresses on the still newer *self-consciousness*[1] its distinctive modern meaning.

Though these two developments—the birth of an historical sense and the birth of our modern self-consciousness —may seem at first sight to have little connection with one another, yet it is not difficult, on further consideration, to perceive that they are both connected with that other and larger process which has already been pointed to as the story told by the history of the Aryan languages as a whole. If we wished to find a name for it, we should have to coin some such ugly word as 'internalization'. It is the shifting of the centre of gravity of consciousness from the cosmos around him into the personal human being himself. The results are twofold: on the one hand the peculiar freedom of mankind, the *spontaneous*[2] impulseswhich control human behaviour and destiny, are felt to arise more and more from *within* the individual, as we saw in the semantic change of such words as *conscience, disposition, spirit, temper,* . . . in the application to inner processes of words like *dissent, gentle, perceive, religion*, and in the Protestant Reformation; on the other the spiritual life and activity felt to be immanent in the world outside—in star and planet, in herb and animal, in the juices and 'humours' of the body, and in the outward ritual of the Church—these grow feebler. The conception of 'laws' governing this world arises and grows steadily more impersonal; words like *consistency, pressure, tension,* . . . are found to describe matter 'objectively' and disinterestedly, and at the same time the earth ceases to be the centre round which the cosmos revolves. All this time the European

[1] The adjective *self-conscious* was first used by Coleridge.
[2] First used by Hobbes in 1656.

171

'ego' appears to be engaged, unawares, in disentangling itself from its environment—becoming less and less of the actor, more and more of both the author and the spectator. In the eighteenth century the word *outlook* is used for the first time in the sense in which it has been used here; in the nineteenth *environment* is introduced by Carlyle. And so it goes on; and as, on the one hand, it is only when that detachment has progressed to a certain point that man becomes able to observe the changes which constitute history, so it is only as he begins to observe them that he becomes fully conscious of himself—the observer.

Thus, the general process which we have called 'internalization' can be traced working itself out into all kinds of details; not only in that intimate, metaphysical change of outlook which it is so hard for us to realize now that the change has taken place—in the appearance of words betokening a sharper self-consciousness—but also in the moral and personal sphere. We could, for instance, take such a common word as *duty* and mark its expansion of meaning at about the time of Shakespeare. By its derivation it carries the sense of 'owing', and it meant in Chaucer's time an act of obedience which was owed to some other person—usually to a feudal superior.[1] It is not till the close of the sixteenth century that it begins to take on its modern sense of a more or less *abstract* moral obligation—an obligation owed, if to any being, to oneself or to a sort of ideal of manhood—such an ideal, for instance, as is expressed in the word *gentleman*. Later on, as with *conscience*, there is a tendency to personify it. At the beginning of the seventeenth

[1] Thus we still describe certain sums of money as a *duty* on goods, or, in Scotland, as a *feu duty* on land.

century we first find the word *Nature* employed in contexts where medieval writers would certainly have used the single word *God*. *Spontaneous* has already been mentioned, and it is interesting to note a certain tendency, which seems to have been inherent, before Shakespeare's time, in the adjective *voluntary*, to connote disapproval when it was applied to human actions or feelings. Later in the century the word *character*[1] was first used in its modern personal sense by the historian Clarendon.

Students of the period know well the sudden, extraordinary craze for 'character-drawing' which swept over France and England at this time. In France literary 'portraits' of oneself and one's friends were produced in hundreds, the first as a hobby, the second actually as a round game; and Clarendon, whose *History of the Great Rebellion* is a string of such character-studies, was only doing systematically what men like Hall, Overbury, Earle, and others had already done in a more disjointed and dilettante way. To the medieval observer a *person* or a *soul* had been interesting chiefly in its relation to Society, to the Church, to the Cosmos. 'All the personality of man,' said Wyclif, 'standeth in the spirit of him.' But these new writers and their readers were interested in *characters* and *characteristics* for their own sakes. We begin to hear of people's *autographs*, of their *foibles* and their *fortes*; *eccentric* is taken from astronomy and mathematics; the Greek word *idiosyncrasy*—signifying an 'individual mixture' (of 'humours')—is borrowed from Galen; but with the new point of view the astrological and physical meanings of this and other words,

[1] A Greek word; literally a mark 'stamped' or 'impressed' on some yielding material. Shakespeare used it of handwriting.

like *disposition, humour, spirits, temperament, . . .*[1] gradually
fade away, and their modern meanings arise instead. One
relic of these ancient physics, however—the *vapours* which
were supposed to rise into the head from the region of the
stomach—lingered well on into the eighteenth century; and
from the way in which Boswell and Johnson write of their
fits of *melancholy*, it seems that they had just reached a point
at which they could not be sure, from their feelings at any
rate, whether their common malady was physical in its
origin or purely mental.

The same difference is observable in the names for feelings and passions. The nomenclature of the Middle Ages
generally views them from without, hinting always at their
results or their moral significance—*envy, greedy, happy* (i.e.
'lucky'), *malice, mercy, mildheartness, peace, pity,*[2] *remorse,
repentance, rue, sin,* . . . Even the old word *sad* had not long
lost its original sense of 'sated', 'heavy' (which it still retains
in *sad bread*), and *fear* continued for a long time to mean,
not the emotion, but a 'sudden and unexpected event'.
Hardly before the beginning of the seventeenth century do
we find expressed that sympathetic or 'introspective' attitude to the feelings which is conveyed by such labels as
aversion, dissatisfaction, discomposure, . . . while *depression* and
emotion—further lenient names for human weaknesses—
were used till then of material objects.

In the eighteenth century we notice, as we should expect,
a considerable increase in the number of these words which
attempt to portray character or feeling from within; such
are *apathy, chagrin, diffidence, ennui, homesickness*, together

[1] See pp. 141 and 171.
[2] See p. 128.

with the expression 'the *feelings*', while *agitation, constraint, disappointment, embarrassment, excitement* are transferred from the outer to the inner world. *Outlook*, which meant 'a place from which a good view is obtained', was first employed figuratively by Dr. Young in 1742.

This brings us to another class of words—appropriate enough to the century which produced Berkeley's *Principles of Human Knowledge*—describing external things not objectively, from their own point of view, but purely by the *effects* which they produce on human beings, such, for instance, as *affecting, amusing, boring, charming, diverting, entertaining, enthralling, entrancing, exciting, fascinating, interesting*, and *pathetic* in its modern sense, none of which are found before the seventeenth and only a few before the eighteenth century. These adjectives can be distinguished sharply—indeed they are in a sense the very opposite of those older words, which can also be said, though less accurately, to describe external objects 'from the human point of view'. Thus, when a Roman spoke of events as *auspicious* or *sinister*, or when some natural object was said in the Middle Ages to be *baleful*, or *benign*, or *malign*, a herb to possess such and such a *virtue*, an eye to be *evil*, or the bones of a saint to be *holy*, or even, probably, when Gower wrote:

The day was merry *and* fair *enough,*

it is true that these things were described from the human point of view, but the activity was felt to emanate from the object itself. When we speak of an object or an event as *amusing*, on the contrary, we know that the process indicated by the word *amuse* takes place within ourselves; and this is none the less obvious because some of the adjectives recorded above, such as *charming, enchanting,* and *fascinating,* are the present participles of verbs which formerly did imply genuine, occult activity.

The change is an important one; it is a reverberation into wider and wider circles of the scholastic progress from Realism to Nominalism, and inside the walls of the Church we can perceive the same movement going on at the Reformation in the Protestant and Dissenting tendency to abandon belief in the Real Presence. Perhaps the somersault was turned most neatly by the old Aristotelean word *sub-jective,* which developed in the seventeenth century from its former meaning of 'existing in itself' to the modern one of 'existing in human consciousness'. *Objective* made a similar move in the opposite direction. When using such words as 'progress' and 'develop' in this connection, however, we must remember that the semantic histories of words merely inform us of changes which have actually occurred in a large number of minds or 'outlooks'. They tell us of what is earlier and what is later, but not of truth and error. In this direction all that a knowledge of them can do is to equip us a little better for forming opinions of our own.

At the same time we find a few words to denote the kind of people who are easily 'affected' in this way. *Susceptible* is first found in Clarendon, and in the eighteenth century the words *sensible* and *sensibility* acquire their special sense of 'easily affected' or 'having the emotions easily aroused'; and as this kind of experience grows more familiar, clearer heads become conscious of it, and the new words *sentiment* and *sentimental* appear. *Sentimental,* which was first used in the title of Sterne's *Sentimental Journey,* published in 1768, was found so convenient that the French language borrowed and the German translated it. No doubt these new notions of 'sensibility' and 'sentimentality', of a variety of emotions lying dormant in the bosom and waiting eagerly to be called forth, combined with the recently developed interest in character to produce the curious *personality*, which acquired its modern meaning a few years later and has gone on increasing in popularity ever since.

It is impossible in the short space that is left to us to do justice to that extraordinary interlude in England's literary and social history—the eighteenth century. The age of powder and platitudes, of *charmers* and *swains*; the age of artificial 'ruins' and of ugly shaven heads secretly perspiring under fashionable periwigs; this age seems to us now to have faded away as suddenly and inexplicably as it arose, leaving only the faintest traces upon our language. Those half-hidden vestiges, however—the just slightly different shades of meaning with which sundry familiar words were used a hundred and fifty years ago—sometimes seem to fascinate us by the very paradox of their proximity and elusiveness. We feel that, if we could only bring them out in some way, we might take from them the very form and pressure of the age. And so, when we come across some particularly popular word like *reason* in eighteenth-century literature, we are sometimes tempted to lay down the book, while imagination goes groping vainly round the impenetrable fringe of that mysterious no-man's-land which lies between words and their meanings.

If we would seek for the genesis of the curious clockwork cosmos through which the minds and imaginations of the period seem to have moved with a measure of contentment, we should find it, perhaps, not so very far back in the past. Emotionally, the age was still dominated by a pronounced reaction against religious fanaticism—an attitude we see reflected in the changeable meaning of *enthusiasm*, which in Plato's Greek meant 'possessed by a god'. Spenser uses it in its Greek form in a good sense, but by the end of the seventeenth century we find Henry More writing: 'If ever Christianity be exterminated, it will be by enthusiasm'; and even as late as 1830 a certain zealous, if dogmatic, Churchman thought it worth while to write and publish a *Natural History of Enthusiasm*, in which that folly, especially in its theological aspect, is castigated with appropriate vigour. *Fanatic*, which had also meant 'possessed by a god or demon', underwent the same change of meaning and gave birth to *fanaticism* about the middle of the seventeenth century. *Extravagant*, which had formerly meant 'non-codified', got its new meaning and produced *extravagance*. And the way in which the word *Gothic* was used to describe anything barbarous and uncouth reminds us of how the eighteenth century perceived barbarity and uncouthness in many places where we no longer see it—such as medieval architecture, much of which was pulled down at this time and replaced by buildings which were felt to be more 'correct' and classical.

Intellectually, on the other hand, men's minds seem to have been influenced above all things by that conception of impersonal 'laws' governing the universe which, as we saw in the last chapter, was scarcely apprehended before the previous century. Poets and philosophers alike were delighted by the perfect *order* in which they perceived the cosmos to be arranged. They sought everywhere for ex-

amples of this orderliness. Pope, for instance, praises Windsor Forest on the ground that it is a place:

> *Not Chaos-like together crush'd and bruis'd;*
> *But, as the world, harmoniously confus'd:*
> *Where order in variety we see,*
> *And where, tho' all things differ, all agree.*

This appreciation of Nature's regularity—from which we
do not ourselves so easily derive poetic inspiration—is now
so familiar that it is difficult for us to realize its freshness at
that time. Yet this is unquestionably demonstrated by the
dates at which such crucial words as *arrange, category, classify,*
method, organize, organization, regular, regulate, regularity,
system, systematic, . . . or their modern meanings, appeared
in the language. Only two of these are earlier than the
seventeenth, and most of them are not found till the
eighteenth century. Thus, *arrange* was a military term like
array until that time, and *regular* was only used of monastic
'orders' until the close of the sixteenth century.

It is this universal conformity to laws, then, this perfect
order reigning everywhere undisturbed, which the eighteenth century seems to have had in mind when it used, and
sometimes personified, the word *Reason*. Reason explained
everything.

> *Let godlike Reason from her sovereign throne*
> *Speak the commanding word—I will—and it is done,*

wrote James Thomson, and Pope expressed the same idea
even more slickly when he announced in his *Essay on Man*:
'Whatever is, is right.' Thus, rapt in adoration of the radi-
ant new lady, the poets lost all interest in dame Nature. Only

when she was arranged and regulated and organized into a park or a landscape garden would they consent to have anything to do with her, and then it was chiefly as a foil to the superior attractions of her rival. She became a stage, a 'pleasing' background to a sort of everlasting human boxing-match between reason and 'the passions'; and the dictionary dates from this time our curious custom of describing her face as *scenery*. And then, after having quietly murdered her, poetry proceeded to galvanize the poor corpse into a shameful, marionette-like semblance of life by switching into it that supposititious *personal* sympathy with human affairs which mars so much of the verse of the eighteenth century. We can, however, mark the beginning of this practice at an earlier date.

The word *conscious*, like *consciousness*, was unknown until the seventeenth century, when its newfangledness was ridiculed by Ben Jonson. It is odd, therefore, that the first recorded uses are figurative, applying it to inanimate objects. When we find Denham writing in 1643:

> *Thence to the coverts and the conscious Groves,*
> *The scenes of his past Triumphs and his Loves....*

and Milton a few years later:

> *So all ere day-spring, under conscious Night*
> *Secret they finished ...*

we can almost fancy, by their readiness to seize upon the new word, that our poets were beginning, even so soon, to feel the need of restoring 'subjectively' to external Nature —of 'projecting into' her, as we are now inclined to say—a fanciful substitute for that voluntary life and inner connection with human affairs which Descartes and Hobbes were draining from her in reality. The tendency we can see here, carried to extravagant lengths, at last produced the poetic conventions of the eighteenth century, by which fictitious personality was attributed to every object and idea under the sun. Finally the complicated machinery of classical mythology was applied in the same subjective and purely fanciful way to English society and the English countryside. It is in the same Windsor Forest that we are asked to

> *See Pan with flocks, with fruits Pomona crowned,*
> *Here blushing Flora paints the enamel'd ground,*
> *Here Ceres' gifts in waving prospect stand,*
> *And nodding tempt the joyful reaper's hand.*

At first sight this state of affairs looks like an exact repetition of the later stages of Roman mythology, but in point of fact the two outlooks are sharply distinguished by the new element of self-consciousness. Myth was in some way in the blood of the Romans; it was a living part of their national history, and in spite of all their artificiality and scepticism there is no evidence that they ever deliberately created gods and goddesses of the fancy, in whom they neither believed themselves nor expected anyone else to believe. We imagine them incapable of grasping, for instance, such an idea as that which found expression in the brand-new eighteenth-century verb, to *personify*. One wonders, therefore, to what extent the dawn of a mechanical age was reflecting itself in this new outlook, this new cosmos controlled by dead laws rather than instinct with living spirit, and therefore requiring to be peopled by the fancy.

We have spoken of the eighteenth-century mind as living in a 'clockwork' cosmos, and it is interesting to reflect that even this simplest form of mechanical contrivance was a thing quite unknown to the ancient world. Was the rhythmical mimicry of organic life, which is the characteristic of machinery, already having its unperceived effect on men's minds and philosophies? The influences which go to make up the outlook of an age are sometimes seen working most powerfully—though beneath the surface—in the very minds which believe themselves to be combating that outlook most stubbornly. The closing years of the eighteenth century produced Paley's famous watch, a popular cosmic allegory which, in proving the existence of a Creator, at the same time relegated all His activities to the remote past. But this is a subject which can be more usefully considered in the next chapter. Thither we must now turn in order to trace the further development of the eighteenth-century gentleman's imaginative double life—his life in the order and reason of the moral and material universe and of 'sensibility' in the little universe of himself—into two divergent directions.

X

MECHANISM

AUTOMATIC · SPRING · SPECIES · CAUSE · AGNOSTIC
UNCTION · SPIRITUALISM · HUMANITARIANISM

The material universe is the complement of the intellect, and without the study of its laws reason would never have awoke to its higher forms of self-consciousness at all. It is the non-ego, through and by which the ego is endowed with self-discernment.—TYNDALL: *Fragments of Science.*

Whatever else a child may be, in respect of this particular question [respiration], it is a complicated piece of mechanism, built up out of materials supplied by its mother; and in the course of such building-up, provided with a set of motors—the muscles. Each of these muscles contains a stock of substance capable of yielding energy under certain conditions, one of which is a change of state in the nerve fibres connected with it. The powder in a loaded gun is such another stock of substance capable of yielding energy in consequence of a change of state in the mechanism of the lock. . . .

The infant is launched into altogether new surroundings; and these operate through the mechanism of the nervous machinery, with the result that the potential energy of some of the work-stuff in the muscles which bring about inspiration is suddenly converted into actual energy; and this, operating through the mechanism of the respiratory apparatus, gives rise to an act of inspiration. As the bullet is propelled by the 'going-off' of the powder, so it might be said that the ribs are raised and the midriff depressed by the 'going-off' of certain portions of muscular work-stuff.—HUXLEY: *Science and Morals.*

The two most interesting points about the passage quoted above from *Science and Morals* are firstly, that it was written, not by an engineer, but by a natural scientist; and secondly, that the title of the essay from which it is taken is *Capital and Labour*. That is to say, the abundance of mechanical simile in it is neither the natural colouring of an imagination subdued to what it works in, nor a deliberate system of metaphors fabricated with the object of figuring forth a biological process to the uninitiated. On the contrary, the notion of child-birth is itself only introduced for the purpose of illustration. The images by which it is conveyed are thus revealed as the natural furniture of the writer's imagination. They can no longer have been images to him, but rather his normal outlook on the chain of facts in which he was most interested; and the passage is, of course, only one of thousands in which we can see nineteenth-century imagination working in a similar way.

It would be of small general interest to give a list of all the mechanical and technical words which had come into our vocabulary since the middle of the seventeenth century —words like *calculus, centrifugal, dynamic, galvanize, inertia, momentum, oscillate, polarity, reciprocating, rotate, vibrate* (except in the sense 'to brandish'),[1] . . . We are concerned more with their influence on the meanings of older words. And from this point of view the passage quoted from Huxley can indeed give us a fair idea of the untold changes that were secretly brewing when, for instance, the word *mechanic* (Greek 'mēchanē', a 'device', or 'contrivance')

[1] Used once in 1632 of sea-waves.

lost its old meaning of 'pertaining to manual labour', and began to be applied to machines. This happened in the seventeenth century, when also the word *machine*, which had formerly been used of plots and intrigues, or for anything erected or put together by man, was first used with its modern meaning. We begin to hear of the six 'Mechanick Faculties' or 'Simple Machines', i.e. the *Balance, Lever, Pulley, Screw, Wedge*, and *Wheel*; and in a little book called *Mathematicall Magick*, by Bishop Wilkins, one of the first members of the Royal Society, these are discussed with great enthusiasm and many respectful references to Aristotle. It is in the same work that we first hear in English of a science of *Mechanics*. This new science, foreshadowed to some extent by Aristotle, from whose treatise with that title we take the word, had quickly been carried farther by his successor, Archimedes. Most civilizations seem to have produced towards their close mechanical devices of one kind or another, but more especially 'engines' of war. What distinguishes our own is the way in which mechanism has gradually entered into our outlook—a fact which is marked, among other things, by our use of the Greek prefix 'auto-' (self) for things worked by machinery. In a Greek dictionary we find upwards of two hundred words beginning with this prefix, but not one of them is applied to anything mechanical.

Let us consider the word *automatic*. The Greek 'automatos', which meant 'self-moved',[1] was Latinized in the form 'automatus' at about the beginning of our era, and

[1] Or 'self-minded'. Its earliest appearance is in Homer's *Iliad*, where it occurs twice, and is applied to divine phenomena, viz. the gates of heaven and the tripod of the god Hephaestus.

automatous—now obsolete—is actually found in the works of the seventeenth-century writer, Sir Thomas Browne. This old adjective had the sense of 'spontaneous', 'of one's own free will', and was used of the animal and vegetable worlds as opposed to the mineral, or of events which came about 'by chance'; while in Plato's philosophy the distinction between that which is 'self-moved', and that which can only be moved by something outside itself had been taken as the very antithesis between spirit and matter, between eternal and perishable. *Automatic* is first found in English in the eighteenth century. The earliest quotation given by the *Oxford Dictionary* is taken from David Hartley, who wrote in 1748:

'The motions of the body are of two kinds, automatic and voluntary. The automatic motions are those which arise from the mechanism of the body in an evident manner. They are called automatic from their resemblance to the motions of automata, or machines, whose principle of motion is within themselves. Of this kind are the motions of the heart and peristaltic motion of the bowels.'

In 1802 Paley pointed out 'the difference between an animal and an automatic statue', and sixty years later a writer on physics, after speaking of the amoeba as being 'irritable and automatic', added a note to the effect that—

'Automatic . . . has recently acquired a meaning almost exactly opposite to that which it originally bore, and an automatic action is now by many understood to mean nothing more than an action produced by some machinery or other. In this work I use it in the older sense, as denoting an action of a body, the causes of which appear to lie in the body itself.'

The reason for this semantic *volte face* may perhaps be detected in the history of the parallel word *automaton*. This had long ago (about 10 B.C.) been applied to the few primitive mechanical devices which Aryan civilization had then evolved, and its appearance in English seems to have preceded that of *automatic* by nearly two centuries, as it is found in 1611 describing 'a picture of a gentlewoman' made with eyes that open and shut. Then, later on in the same century, it began to be applied to clocks and watches, and there seems every reason to suppose that the presence of this particular kind of apparent 'self-mover' on so many mantelpieces and in so many vest-pockets must have determined the peculiarly dead and mechanical meaning which *automatic* now possesses.

The ancients measured time by the regulated flow of water. Striking clocks of some kind were known in Europe as far back as the twelfth or thirteenth century. But they seem to have been unreliable, costly, and rare until the discovery by Galileo of the 'isochronism' of pendulums. *Pendulum* is first found in 1660, in Boyle's writings, *vibrate* and *vibration* in 1667. The new toy seems to have taken hold of Europe's imagination in the most extraordinary way. Both *clockwork* and *mainspring* were used figuratively the first time they are known to have been used in English at all, a sixteenth-century writer even anticipating Paley so far as to write:

> *God's the main spring, that maketh every way*
> *All the small wheels of this great Engin play.*

We hear talk almost at once of the *springs*[1] of people's actions. Descartes compared the souls of brutes to watches, and Leibnitz actually compared the souls and bodies of men to *two* watches! It seems as though the works had started going in our heads.

And since then, so far from stopping, they have accelerated, especially during the last century—to what extent it is difficult for us to realize fully, simply because it has all happened so recently. Differences of outlook on such matters as biology and physiology between ourselves and the Middle Ages we readily perceive, though we may not properly understand them; here we stand a long way off, and can often see quite plainly how the old words have altered their meanings. But from the way in which our great grandfathers used such words as *energy, midriff, motor, muscle, nerve, respiration, work*—to take examples only from the passage quoted at the beginning of this chapter—we sometimes find it hard, even when we have traced the history of their meanings up to that date, to feel what different associations they must have called up to the generations which died before Huxley was born. At this time, fifty years after his death, it is only our own imagination, working introspectively on such a phrase as 'nervous machinery', and grasping, as it can do, how the meanings of the two words have been running into one another, which can bring this difference before us. When it has done so, we are again reminded of the simple yet striking truth that all knowledge which has been conveyed by means of speech to the reason has travelled in metaphors taken from

[1] The meaning of this metaphor has probably been affected by the other meaning of *spring* (as in *well-spring*), but this did not occur till later.

man's own activities and from the solid things which he handles. The present is no different from the past. Only the metaphors get buried deeper and deeper beneath one another; they interact more subtly, and do not always leave any *outward* trace on the language. It would be interesting, for example, were it possible, to discover just how much of the average man's idea of blood circulation is due to the invention of that elementary mechanical device, the pump;[1] or how much of the mental image which he has formed of the interaction of muscle, nerve, and brain would fade from his consciousness if there were no such thing as the electric telegraph.

We think by means of words, and we have to use the same ones for so many different thoughts that, as soon as new meanings have entered into one set, they creep into all our theories and begin to mould our whole cosmos; and from the theories they pass into more words, and so into our lives and institutions. Thus, not only were the Newtonian heavens the playground of just those forces which had been used for the working of the six 'simple machines', but Montesquieu insists that the English Whigs copied the new astronomy when they were creating the modern British Constitution. Referring to this in one of his essays,

[1] Not only is the word *pump* constantly used to describe the heart's action, but one must also consider its reaction on the meaning of older physiological terms such as *valve*. *Pump*, with the meaning 'ship's pump', is found in English in the fifteenth century, but in the sense of 'instrument for raising water' it is unknown to the Teutonic languages before the sixteenth century, though instruments of some sort had been used for that purpose in classical times. An understanding of the underlying mechanical principle, however, only developed, as we should expect, in the seventeenth century, when the words *suction* and *hydraulic* appeared in, for instance, Bacon's writings. Harvey published his treatise, *De motu cordis et sanguinis*, in 1628.

Woodrow Wilson drew attention to the fact that the Constitution of the United States had been made on the same principle. 'They [writers in the *Federalist*] speak of the *checks* and *balances* of the Constitution,' he said, 'and use to express their idea the simile of the organization of the universe, and particularly of the solar system. . . .' And we notice that the President himself, when he went on to speak of reconstructing the Constitution, was fain to lean on another analogy, reminding his hearers that government is 'not a machine, but a living thing'; that it is 'modified by its environment, necessitated by its tasks, shaped to its functions by the sheer pressure of life'; and again that it is a body of men 'with highly differentiated functions'. In fact, we are merely launched into another set of metaphors, of which, however, the speaker is in this case conscious, for he explicitly affirms that government is 'accountable to Darwin, not to Newton'.

Environment, evolution, development, instinct, species, spontaneous, variation are some of the more important words, whose modern meanings, if we look at their semantic history, are found to bear the unmistakable stamp of Darwinism, and we ought perhaps to add *ooze*[1] and *slime*.[1] To Darwin we should have to attribute the tendency of *evolution* to lose its etymological suggestion of a vegetable growth, an unfolding from the centre outwards. *Species* (Latin 'species', 'form' 'or appearance') was used by Cicero to translate Plato's 'Idea' (Chapter VI). It held an

---

[1] Especially in conjunction with such epithets as *primeval* or *primal*, in which combination these words have frequently been made to bear a considerable part of the suggestiveness and meaning long ago worked into such words as *creation, mystery, sacrament, the Word*, . . . (see previous chapters).

important place in the logic of the Middle Ages as one of the five 'predicables' by which an object could be defined, and for centuries its biological meaning was only one among many. This particular interpretation did not begin to come into prominence until the eighteenth century, when Addison, for instance, used the phrase 'the species' of the human race; but since Darwin published his *Origin of Species* (in which the word is, of course, given an exclusively biological sense) it has, for the ordinary man, had practically no other. It is interesting to observe, that here again, as the words are commonly employed, the Latin form has grown more concrete and the Greek more abstract and intellectual.

But the change did not confine itself to such technical words as these. One has only to pick up a journalistic article on almost any subject and read it, endeavouring to let the words mean only what they did a hundred years ago, to see how the whole scheme of Natural Selection can lurk unseen, but not unfelt, behind some colourless little word like *adapt, competition, gregarious, modification, protective, selection*, and even *animal, facts, law, life, man, Nature*, . . . Or we can see it in the curious, absolute use of the word *fit*, in the sense of 'physically healthy', which, appearing first in the seventies, is obviously due to the famous phrase, the 'survival of the fittest' (i.e. the fittest to survive in a struggle for existence). How modern the new meanings are may be gauged by the fact that the word *heredity*, the basic principle of modern natural scientific theory, is recorded by Francis Galton as having been considered 'fanciful and unusual' in 1859, while *atavism* first appears in 1833.

Now that a little more time has elapsed and the nineteenth century can be properly studied from the semantic point of view, it may begin to dawn on us that the inter-fusion of mechanical and biological conceptions and the penetration of both into meaning presents one of its most striking features. One of the greatest triumphs of mechanism—greater than the Forth Bridge or the St. Gothard Tunnel—is the fact that it has wormed itself into the meaning of the word *cause*. This is, of course, a word which tends to alter its meaning a little every time it is used, and there is evidence that in former times, while there were separate words to express such separate ideas as 'bringing to birth', 'making to grow', 'being guilty of', . . . there was no general term into which one single essence supposed to be common to all these relations had been dis-tilled. The Greek and Latin words for *cause*, for example, were both closely connected from the earliest times with their legal procedure (cf. *ac-cuse*, etc., and the modern use of *cause* in the same sense). At some period, however—per-haps in the last two centuries before our era—such a con-cept must have been precipitated, and we find Cicero defining the Latin 'causa', with mathematical precision, simply as 'that which effects the thing of which it is the cause'. The fascination which this abstraction exerted on the medieval imagination may be judged from the fact that the writer of a fifteenth-century treatise on Love intro-duced into it the sentence: 'Every cause of a cause is cause of thing caused'; and we soon find the philosophers seeking through a 'chain' of causes for that First Cause, which they identified with the Almighty. By the nineteenth century this thought-system of an abstract *causality*, brought about by means of abstract 'laws', lay, like an empty house, ready to be taken over by a new owner. The new owner was mechanism.

'The great abstract law of mechanical causality' (mechanische Kausalität), wrote Haeckel in 1899, 'now rules the entire universe, as it does the mind of man. It is the steady, immutable pole-star, whose clear light falls on our path through the dark labyrinth of the countless separate phenomena.'

Under its influence even consciousness itself was, and still is, often conceived of as being *caused* by mechanical movements taking place within the body. We also find thought described as a *function* of the brain. This curious word had become extremely popular; and somewhere about the sixties the noun began to be used as a verb. We hear of nerves, brain, heàrt, . . . *functioning* or refusing to *function*, an expression in which the mechanical flavour is especially strong.

Thus, in the light of words, the historical relation between mechanics and physiology looks not unlike that relation between mathematics and astronomy which was suggested in a previous chapter. We drew from out our own bodies, it would seem, the sense-experiences of *force* and *pressure* and the like,[1] on which mechanics are based; then we externalized them in tools and machines, and turned them into abstract 'laws'; finally, we proceeded to reapply the 'laws' to the familiar objects from which we had first extracted them, and the result was that we turned our previous notions of these inside out. For the typical intellectual position towards the end of the nineteenth century

[1] See p. 165.

was exactly the reverse of the typical Academic position. Plato had deduced the sense-world from what we have called the inner world, and, while he had worked out an elaborate and wise knowledge of this inner world, with its moral impulses and aspirations, his philosophy had remained admittedly bankrupt as far as detailed knowledge of the mechanism of the outer world was concerned. Nineteenth-century science, on the other hand, deduced the inner from the outer; it had mapped and charted the mechanical part of Nature to a tenth of a millimetre,[1] but it was wellnigh bankrupt as far as the inner world was concerned. Huxley invented the word *agnostic* (not-knowing) to express his own attitude, and that of many millions since his day, to the nature and origin of all this part of the cosmos. One of the few things about which practically all 'men of science', as the phrase now went, besides all those laymen who took the trouble to follow out the various scientific discoveries and to listen to their metaphysical reverberations, were agreed upon was that his senses and his reason had succeeded in placing man in a material environment which appeared to bear no relation whatever to his inner feelings and moral impulses.

For the expression of these, his proper humanity, he continued, irrespective of his conscious belief, to live on what had been developed through Plato and the Gospels, the Church and the poets. For it was these, as we have seen, which had built up the meanings of those old words in

[1] Of English words beginning with 'iso-'—a Greek prefix meaning 'of equal measurement' (*isosceles*, 'equal legged', *isobar*, 'equal pressure', . . .), about twelve came in before the nineteenth century, about seventy in the course of it.

terms of which he learnt to think and feel about his fellow-men. Whenever the biologico-mechanical meanings did creep into human relationships—as, for example, into the economic relationship through the word *competition* and otherwise—the result was, almost without exception, disastrous. The famous Encyclical Letter and Syllabus of 1864, in which modern movements of thought were condemned and anathematized wholesale from the Vatican, was thus in some sense an attempt to express in dogmatic form a principle which was, in fact, already active throughout Europe. And the pathetic impotence of this papal gesture probably marks the maximum point of that divergence between science and religion, as modes of experience, which first became noticeable in the Alexandrian world, and of which nineteenth-century philosophy had become sufficiently conscious to create the word *Dualism*.

The rapid conquest of intellectual Europe, which was achieved, not only by the general idea of evolution, but by the particular Darwinian theory of mechanical natural selection, is a matter of some surprise when we consider that a full acceptance of it necessitated a reversal of practically every metaphysical idea and feeling likely to be present in a nineteenth-century soul. No doubt one could point to a variety of causes. There is evidence, for instance, in a certain class of word which had recently begun to multiply that even in Protestant countries the custodians of the ancient outlook were not always fortresses of wisdom and enlightenment. *Religionism* appears towards the close of the eighteenth century, and then *religiosity* (in a bad sense),[1] and in the next century the now obsolete *religiose*. The

[1] Wyclif had used it in a good sense.

word *pious*, which had long been degenerating towards an imputation of feeble-mindedness, formed an unpleasant derivative, *pietism*, which in turn produced its adjective *pietistic*; and in 1864—an appropriate year—we first come up against *clericalism*. *Unction*—the name of one of the deepest mysteries of the Catholic Church—is first recorded by the *Oxford English Dictionary* with an offensive meaning in 1870, when Lowell writes of 'that clerical unction which in a vulgar nature so easily degenerates into greasiness'. *Unctuous* was not long in following suit, and instances could no doubt be multiplied. The extension towards the priesthood of this particular shade of disapproval seems to have been the product of the age. Possibly the single earlier example is the old word *cant*, which dates back to the Middle Ages, and is said to have been born of exasperation at the whining tone adopted by the mendicant friars in their 'chants' (cantare). In the same way may we not suppose that the words quoted above grew up out of that extraordinary atmosphere of partly bovine, partly hypocritical, acquiescence in unexamined dogma which Stuart Mill hit off in his famous phrase?[1]

Nevertheless, we should have to look deeper than all this for the true causes of a change of outlook as rapid and emphatic as that which swept through the last century. If we did so, we should probably discern, as one of the most efficient, that vivid sense of orderliness and *arrangement* which had grown up during the eighteenth century, the reverence for Reason, and especially for Reason reflected[2]

---

[1] 'There is no God—but this is a family secret'.

[2] Huxley, in whose imagination was to some extent epitomized what was proceeding in varying degrees of intensity in minds all over Europe, describes Nature as a 'materialized logical process'.

in the impartial laws which govern the working of Nature. To minds thus attuned direct intervention by the divine at any one point in the natural process could only seem like an intolerable liberty; and feeling as well as thought began to revolt at the conjuring-tricks apparently reported in the Gospels. Perhaps there is a faint indication of the new point of view in the nineteenth-century use of the word *freak* to describe a *lusus naturae*, instead of the old *monster*, which is derived from the Latin 'moneo' and implies that the oddity is sent as a divine warning or portent.

The new cosmos—a complex of matter and forces proceeding mechanically from spiral nebula to everlasting ice —took such a firm hold on the imagination of Europe that labels like *spiritualism, spiritualist, spiritualistic*[1] were employed to describe those who believed it was anything more, and even *Vitalism* and *Vitalist* to distinguish those who held that life, as such, had any purpose or significance. It is a curious remark that the erection within men's imaginations of this severely mechanical framework for themselves was accompanied by, and may have been partly responsible for, an increase in their sense of self-consciousness. The more automatic the cosmos, apparently, the more the vital ego must needs feel itself detached. At any rate, we find upwards of forty words hyphened with *self* created in the nineteenth century, and of these only about six (*self-*

---

[1] *Spiritualist*, however, is found as early as the middle of the seventeenth century; but it was employed in the sense of 'fanatical', etc., or with the more technical meaning of 'one who supports ecclesiastical authority'. Its use as a purely philosophical designation seems to date from about the middle of the nineteenth century, and the modern 'table-rapping' implication is later still. There is now a tendency to substitute *spiritism, spiritist*, . . . in the latter sense.

acting, self-regulating, . . .) are mechanical. Nor was it only the material world from which men felt themselves more aloof. Herbert Spencer remarked on the recent extension of the meaning of the word *phenomenon* to cover the thoughts of human beings—a point of view which suggests an increased degree of detachment even from thought itself; and an enormous number of words with terminations such as *-ism, -ist, -ite, -ology, -arian,* are indications of a more contemplative attitude to all that we ourselves do and feel and think. What a difference between being *feminine* and being a *feminist,* between *hope* and *optimism, romance* and *romanticism,* between *Christianity* and *Christology,* between liking *vegetables* and being a *vegetarian*! We are hardly conscious at all of being *human,* more so of being *humane,* more still of being *humanitarian,* and very conscious indeed of *humanitarianism.*

Detachment, however, spells freedom; and words are not wanting to remind us of that enhanced sense of the value of individual liberty which now found expression in the writings of the great Romantics and of men like John Stuart Mill. *Autonomy* had not been applied to individuals, but only to states and societies, until the close of the eighteenth century, and in the following century the adjective *autonomous* was introduced. We may compare *liberalism* and *liberal-minded* with the old *libertine; authoritarian* implies a feeling in him who uses the word that all authority, as such, is bad; the nineteenth century also saw the distinction between *broad-minded* and *narrow-minded,* and between *obscurantism* and *enlightenment*—a word which met with some opposition, according to FitzEdward Hall, who records in his *Modern English* (1873) that:

'Enlightenment is, to this day, always used by a certain class of English writers with a manifest sneer. The writers referred to are those who would rather have been born under the rule of the barons than under the inchoate rule of reason, and would gladly exchange the age of science for the ages of faith and folly. Those who object to the word will ordinarily be found to object to all that it stands for.'

Since the sense of freedom often appeared at its strongest in imaginations which were most possessed with the mechanical view of the universe, the paradox was not infrequent —especially in Germany—of philosophers and scientists insisting fiercely on the freedom of thought and using it to deny the possibility of any freedom at all! Such thinkers found the word *Determinism* useful to express the mechanical part of the old *predestination* without the latter's theological assumptions.

Other words which seem to be connected with the same trend of thought are those that confine themselves to expressing a sense of the worth and dignity of man, *as* man, and irrespective of his cosmic connections. Such are *humanism*,[1] *humanitarian*,[1] *humanitarianism, individualism, individualist, individualistic*, and many of the *self* words, such as Carlyle's *self-help*, or the semantic change of *self-respect*, which is first recorded as used with a praiseworthy meaning in Wordsworth's *Prelude*. Now the consciousness of the absolute value and infinite potentiality of each human soul is revealed, as we saw, by the words in which it first began to take verbal form, as having been essentially an attribute of Christianity. Yet how differently these nineteenth-cen-

[1] Both these words referred at the time of their introduction to the new doctrine that Christ was a merely human figure.

tury words sound from the Christian vocabulary of the human and social virtues—*charity, lovingkindness, mercy, pity,* and the like! The modern words seem to be related to these glowing old Christian terms as the unemphasized, because unquestioned, mutual affection of a happy couple is related to the voluble ardours of courting. They preserve, we may say—they have even greatly developed—that divine sense of the value and autonomy of each individual human soul. But it is now more of a *political* autonomy. It is as though they respected it rather from a manly sense of obligation, and the sense of obligation is even extended, as we see in the later semantic development of *humane, humanity,* and *humanitarian,* to the brutes.

Thus, if the one outlook is indeed a lineal descendant of the other, we are constrained to ask a little sadly what had become of a certain sunny element, a suppressed poetic energy, a wonder and a wild surprise, which lurks in the former words, but somehow—with all our respect for them—not in the latter. And for light upon this question we must turn to yet another group of words—small, yet of such far-reaching implications as to demand a final chapter to themselves.

XI

IMAGINATION

ART · FICTION · CREATIVE · GENIUS · ROMANTIC
FANCY · IMAGINATION · DREAM

Early Christianity, with its delighted recognition of the soul's reality, its awful consciousness of inner depths unplumbed, had produced, as we saw, many words describing human emotions by their *effects*, and especially by their effects on the soul's relation to the Divine. In the sixteenth and seventeenth centuries, with the increase of self-consciousness among the leisured classes, a more sympathetic, 'introspective'[1] attitude to the emotions grew up, and this we traced to its development in the romantic *sensibility* of the seventeenth and eighteenth centuries. How did it fare, then, with this tender nursling in the years that followed? Was it crushed and dissected into a neatly labelled little corpse, or was it suffered to grow up unchecked, uneducated, into the middle-aged and well-fed *sentimentalism* of our Victorian ancestors? Fortunately it avoided both these fates. Carefully tended by small groups of earnest men, now in this academy and now in that, it had escaped the dissection of Nature because it had learned not

[1] 1820; but *introspection* was given its modern meaning by Dryden.

to draw its nourishment from Nature and the God of Nature, but from man himself. And on this diet it had thriven and waxed until it was a veritable young giant, able to stand up and confront Nature as her equal. But we must retrace our steps a little.

Attentive readers of Jane Austen's novels will have noticed the slightly unfamiliar way in which she employs the two words *romantic* and *picturesque*. A closer examination reveals the fact that in her time they still bore traces of their origin. These adjectives are taken from the arts, *romantic* meaning in the first instance 'like the old Romances', and *picturesque* 'like a picture' or 'reminding one of a picture'. They are thus members of a quite considerable group of words and phrases, *attitude, comic, dramatic, lyrical, melodramatic, point of view*, and the like, in which terms taken in the first place from the arts are subsequently applied to life. Nowadays we sometimes go farther and use the name of a particular artist, speaking, for instance, of a *Turneresque* sunset, a *Praxitelean* shape; or we even call to our aid a writer's fictitious creatures, as in '*Falstaffian* morality', 'the *Pickwickian* sense', ... Such a figure of speech looks at first sight like any other kind of imagery, and we perhaps imagine it in use since the beginnings of art. In point of fact, however, it is probable that it was not known before the time of the Renaissance, when men's notions of art changed so suddenly, when, indeed, their very consciousness of it as a separate, unrelated activity, something which can be distinguished in thought from a 'craft', a 'trade', or a religious ceremony, seems to have first sprung into being. Moreover, the ancient word *art* used to include in its purview not only these meanings, but also most of those which we now group under the heading *science*. In the Middle Ages the Seven Liberal Arts[1]— *Grammar, Logic, Rhetoric, Arithmetic, Geometry, Music,* and *Astronomy*—were contrasted with the 'servile' or 'mechanical' arts—that is, handicrafts involving manual labour. And thus, though *art* in this wide sense is old, *artist* first occurs in Sir Philip Sidney's *Apologie for Poetry. Artisan* appeared at about the same time, and was not then, as now, confined to mechanical and manual labourers.

> *O, what a world of profit and delight*

wrote the poet, Marlowe,

> *Is promis'd to the studious artisan.*

In the light of two or three familiar words let us try and trace the development, from Sidney's time onwards, of some of our modern notions of 'art', and in particular of poetry. Criticism—the branch of literature or journalism with which our daily and weekly reviews make us so familiar—does not date very far back into the past. Its parents were the medieval arts of grammar and philology, which, among the commentators on classical texts, had already sometimes blossomed into the rudiments of aesthetic. The actual words *critic* and *critical*, however, have been traced no farther back than Shakespeare; *critic* in its aesthetic sense is first found in Bacon; and *criticism* and *criticize* are neither of them earlier than the seventeenth century. Based for the most part on Aristotle's *Poetics*, serious criticism began to take shape in England at the Renaissance. From

[1] Hence the titles of our University Degrees—*Bachelor of Arts, Master of Arts,* . . .

Elizabethan critical essays, such as Sidney's *Apologie for Poetry*, we can get an idea of the light in which poetry and the other arts had begun to be viewed at that time. To Sidney, for example, the distinguishing mark of poetry was, not metre, but a certain 'feigning'. The first philosophers and historians, he affirmed, were also poets, not indeed because of what we should magnificently call their 'creative imagination', but simply because they 'invented' certain fictitious persons and events. We should not now regard this as a virtue in an historian. Sidney, however, points out the derivation of *poetry* from the Greek 'poiein', 'to make',[1] and shows how this distinguishes it from all the other arts and sciences, which in the last analysis merely 'follow Nature', while only the poet,

'disdaining to be tied to any such subjection, lifted with the vigour of his own invention, doth grow in effect another nature, in making things either better than Nature bringeth forth, or, quite anew, forms such as never were in Nature, as the Heroes, Demigods, Cyclops, Chimeras, Furies, and such like: so as he goeth hand in hand with Nature, not enclosed within the narrow warrant of her gifts, but freely ranging only within the Zodiac of his own wit.'

And Sidney adds that this fact is not to be made light of merely because the works of Nature are 'essential' while the poet's are only 'in imitation or fiction'. The poet has contemplated the 'Ideas' behind Nature, and it is those which he 'delivers forth, as he hath imagined them'. With

---

[1] Poets were regularly called *makers* in the fourteenth and fifteenth centuries. 'I know not', says Sidney, 'whether by luck or wisdom we Englishmen have met with the Greeks in calling him a "maker".'

ten or twenty new novels appearing on the bookstalls every week it is not so easy for us to realize the dignity and glory which were once felt to distinguish this great human achievement of *fiction*—that is, of 'making' or 'making up' (from the Latin 'fingere', to 'form' or 'make') purely imaginary forms, instead of merely copying Nature.

Now the presence of a made-up element, especially when it comprised supernatural beings such as giants and fairies, was held to be one of the distinguishing marks of a *romance*. The old medieval romances, as their name suggests, had been nursed to life in that curious period of contact between Roman and Celtic myth which also gave us such words as *fairy* and *sorcery*.[1] They were so called because they were written or recited in the *romance* vernacular[2] instead of in literary Latin, and they seem to have developed out of an increasing tendency among the medieval bards to embroider, on their own responsibility, the traditional accounts of historical and mythical events. This tendency, wherever it had hitherto been detected among the western Aryans, had been strenuously opposed in the interests of learning and morality. It was one of the reasons why Plato decided to expel poets from his Republic, and it is remarkable that the earlier uses of a word like *fable* in twelfth- and thirteenth-century French and fourteenth-century English should have been all condemnatory. Now by the time the Renaissance dawned on England this word had come to be applied, in one instance at least, not merely to the embroidery, but to the garment itself, so that, for example, the whole prodigious fabric of classical mythology might be implicit in the disparaging phrase 'fables of

[1] See pp. 93-94.   [2] See p. 45.

poets'. And after the Revival of Learning, when the most able men began to have a very different feeling towards the myths of Greece and Rome, such a phrase became the very opposite of disparaging. *Fiction* and *romance* were gradually recognized as a legitimate and noble expression of the human spirit.

Gradually: to Sidney, poetry was still, after Aristotle's definition, 'an art of imitation'; only poets must 'to imitate, borrow nothing of what is, hath been, or shall be, but range . . . into the divine consideration of what may be and should be'. And during the seventeenth century all art continued to be regarded as imitation, of which, however, there were two kinds—the imitation of other arts and the imitation of Nature herself. The second kind, by analogy from picture-dealing, was called *original*, and the faculty which achieved it was named *invention* (Latin, 'invenire', 'to find'), a word implying that something had been found in Nature which had not *yet* been imitated by man. Early in the eighteenth century the substantive *originality* was formed from *original*, and an increasing importance began to be attached to the element of novelty in experiences of all kinds, Addison placing it on a level with greatness and beauty as a source of pleasure to the imagination.

At the same time another word appeared in the vocabulary of aesthetic criticism. An Elizabethan critic had already pointed out that, if poets could indeed spin their poetry entirely out of themselves, they were as '*creating* gods', and Dryden soon used the same verb of Shakespeare, because, in Caliban, he had *invented* 'a person not in Nature'. So also Addison:

'. . . this Talent, of affecting the Imagination . . . has something in it like Creation: It bestows a kind of Existence, and draws up to the Reader's View several Objects which are not to be found in Being. It makes Additions to Nature, and gives greater Variety to God's Works.'

This word, too, with its derivative *creative*, is used far too often and too lightly[1] now to allow us to easily perceive its importance. 'Creare' was one of those old Latin words which had been impregnated through the Septuagint and the Vulgate with Hebraic and Christian associations; its constant use in ecclesiastical Latin had saturated it with the special meaning of *creating*, in divine fashion, out of nothing, as opposed to the merely human *making*, which signified the rearrangement of matter already created, or the imitation of 'creatures'. The application of such a word to human activities seems to mark a pronounced change in our attitude towards ourselves, and it is not surprising that, in the course of its career, the new use should have met with some opposition on the grounds of blasphemy.

Once established, however, the conception evidently reacted on other terms embodying theories of art, such, for example, as *original* and *originality* (already mentioned), *art, artist, genius, imagination, inspiration, poesy, poetry*, and others. The meaning which *inspiration* possessed up to the seventeenth or eighteenth centuries carries us right back to the old mythical outlook in Greece and elsewhere, when poets and prophets were understood to be the direct mouthpieces of superior beings—beings such as the Muses, who

---

[1] London emporiums even advertise themselves in chatty essays entitled *The Creative Aspect of a Store*.

inspired or 'breathed into' them the divine afflatus. Through Plato and Aristotle this conception came to England at the Renaissance and lasted as an element of aesthetic theory well on into the eighteenth century, if it can be said to have died out altogether even now. But, like so many other words, this one began in the seventeenth century to suffer that process which we have called 'internalization'. Hobbes poured etymologically apposite scorn on the senseless convention 'by which a man, enabled to speak wisely from the principles of Nature and his own meditation, loves rather to be thought to speak by inspiration, like a Bagpipe'. And we may suppose that from about this time *inspiration*, like some of the 'character' words which we traced in a previous chapter, began to lose its old literal meaning and to acquire its modern and metaphorical one. Like *instinct*, it was now felt, whatever its real nature, to be something arising from within the human being rather than something instilled from without.

Such a revised notion of the immediate source of human activities inevitably concentrated attention on the individual artist—a fact which may perhaps be reflected in the use from the seventeenth century onwards of the word *genius* to describe not merely the 'creative' faculty, but its possessor. For we can speak now of such and such a man being 'a *genius*'. This little word, on which a whole chapter might be written, comes from the Latin 'genius'[1] (from

---

[1] *Demon* is the Greek name for the same being, its present infernal associations having been merely imported by the hostility and superstition of early Christianity. Socrates, for instance, attributed all his wisdom to his 'daimonion', and *genius* must undoubtedly have been affected by this word through the assiduous translation of Greek philosophy into Latin (see p. 101).

'gign-o', 'to bring into being', a stem appearing also in *ingenious, engine*, . . .), which in Roman mythology meant a person's tutelary spirit, or special angel attending him everywhere and influencing his thoughts and actions. Its early meaning in English was much the same as that of *talent*,[1] which, of course, takes its meaning from the New Testament parable. That is to say, *genius* signified an ability implanted in a man by God at his birth. But from about the seventeenth century this meaning began to ferment and expand in the most extraordinary way; it was distinguished from, and even opposed to, *talent*, and in the following century its force and suggestiveness were much enhanced by the use which was made of it to translate the Arabic 'Djinn', a powerful supernatural being. Although nowadays we generally distinguish this particular sense by the spelling *Genie*, the temporary fusion of meanings certainly deepened the strength and mystery of the older word, and may even have procreated the later Byronic tradition of mighty, lonely *poets* with open necks and long hair and a plethora of mistresses and daguerreotypes.

Before, however, these words could acquire the potent meanings which they bear today, they had to run the gauntlet of the Age of Reason, with its hatred of all that savours of enthusiasm and fanaticism. And it was out of the ridicule and distrust which they encountered at its hands that the important new epithet *romantic*, together with some obsolete terms like *romancy, romancical, romantical*, . . . was born. With its meaning of 'like the old romances' (and therefore barbarous, fantastic), *romantic* was one of those adjectives, like *enthusiastic, extravagant, Gothic*, by which the

[1] A Greek monetary unit.

later seventeenth, and the eighteenth century expressed their disapproval of everything which did not bear the stamp of reason and polite society. It was soon applied to people whose heads were stuffed out with the ballooning extravagancies of the old romances, just as *enthusiastic* was employed to describe superstitious people who believed themselves distended with a special variety of divine inspiration. Above all, it had the sense of fabulous, unreal, unnatural. 'Can anything,' asked Bishop South, 'be imagined more profane and impious, absurd, and indeed romantic?' But at the beginning of the eighteenth century this meaning developed a little farther. *Romantic* was now used of places, or aspects of Nature, of the kind among which the old Romances had been set. It was noticed that 'romantic' people displayed a preference for wild landscapes and ruined castles, and would even 'fancy' these things, where more rational people could see nothing more exciting than a tumbledown barn and a dirty ditch. And it is this particular shade of meaning, together with a strong suggestion of absurdity and unreality, which the word seems still to have conveyed to Jane Austen, who preferred to use *picturesque* in contexts where we should now employ *romantic* in its approving or noncommittal sense.

Had one of her heroines, however, succeeded in emerging from that endless round of incredibly dull activities which she contrives to make so incredibly interesting, and had this enterprising young woman then attempted to breast the intellectual currents of the age, she would have been startled to find that that sarcastic consciousness of a war between sense and sensibility, which was her creator's inspiration, was a spent stream flowing from the remote past. For while echoes of the original thinking of men like Bacon, Hobbes, and Locke continued to rumble and reverberate on in the disparaging implications carried by a word like *romantic*, a new note had already become audible beneath them as long ago as the beginning of the century. It was an undertone of reluctant approval. These 'romantic' notions might be absurd, but they were at least pleasant. 'We do not care for seeing through the falsehood', wrote Addison, 'and willingly give ourselves up to so agreeable an imposture.'

It was in the second half of the eighteenth century that this aesthetic[1] vocabulary—*genius, original, romantic, . . .*—whose meanings had up to the present been developed largely by the English, began to make a stir on the Continent. The words were talked of in France; they were taken up by the critics, poets, and philosophers of Germany; and after much handling by men like Kant, Hegel, Schelling, Goethe, and others, the further and partly popularized meanings which they thus acquired were, in a sense, again inserted into their English forms by one or two Englishmen who, towards the close of the century, felt a strong affinity between their own impulses and the *Sturm und Drang* which had been agitating Germany. The most influential of these was Samuel Taylor Coleridge, and just before the turn of the century there burst, with his help, upon England that

---

[1] To the beginning of this period in Germany we owe the word *aesthetic*, which we take from the German philosopher Baumgarten's use of 'aesthetik' to describe a 'criticism of taste' considered as part of a complete philosophy. Needless to say, the word chosen (Greek 'aisthētos', 'perceived by the senses') bears a relation to the nature of Baumgarten's theory.

strange explosion which received, naturally enough, the name of the Romantic Movement. At first it took the form of a sort of cult of the Middle Ages. *Ballad* is another word which added several cubits to its stature by travelling in France and Germany, where it also gave birth to the musical *ballade*; and we find medieval words like *bard, foray, gramarye*[1] (and its Scotch derivative, *glamour*), and *raid*, revived by Walter Scott after having fallen out of use for two or three hundred years. *Derring-do*—another of these revivals—is interesting because it originates in a mistake made by Spenser about Chaucer. He had described how Troilus was second to nobody in 'derring do that longeth to a knight'—that is to say, 'in daring to do that which belongs to a knight'—or, in Cornish idiom, 'that which a knight "belongs to do"'. It is easy to see the nature of Spenser's error. The mysterious substantive *derring-do* (desperate courage), which he created and used several times, is not found again until Scott's *Ivanhoe*.

Very soon the Romantic Movement was resuscitating the Elizabethan world as well as the 'Gothic'—a word, by the way, which now, for the first time in its history, began to connote approval. It was Coleridge himself who invented the word *Elizabethan*, and his inspiring lectures on Shakespeare must be very largely responsible for that renewed and deepened interest in the great dramatist in which Germany once more set us the example. It is also noteworthy that the word *fitful*, which Shakespeare had probably coined in the famous line from *Macbeth*, was never used again until the close of the eighteenth century; and another word which expired when the Elizabethan spirit expired in

[1] See p. 135.

Milton, to be resurrected in the nineteenth century, is *faery*, with that spelling, and with the meaning, not so much of an individual sprite as of a magic realm or state of being—almost 'the whole supernatural element in romance'.

This supernatural element—as we saw in the history of the words *creative* and *genius*—is connected very intimately indeed with the origin of the Romantic Movement. And we shall see the connection even more clearly in the semantic development of two more words—the last to be examined in this book—*fancy* and *imagination*. The various Greek words which the Latin 'imago' was used to translate acquired their special meanings among the Stoics, where, as we saw in Chapter VI, that teasing sense of a contrast, a lack of connection, between the 'objective' and 'subjective' worlds appears first to have developed. One of these words was 'phantasia', from which we have taken indirectly the divergent forms *fantasy*, *phantasy*, and *fancy*. In the first century A.D. the Greek 'phantasia' was predominantly used, so we are told, 'in cases where, carried away by enthusiasm and passion, you think you see what you describe, and you place it before the eyes of your hearers'.[1] 'Phantasia' and 'imaginatio' were in use among the Schoolmen, and *fantasy* and *imagination* are both found in Chaucer in the sense of 'a mental image or reflection', or more particularly 'an image of something which either has no real existence or does not yet exist'. After the Renaissance Shakespeare suddenly transfigured one of the two words in one of those extraordinary passages which make

[1] Longinus, *On the Sublime*, a treatise which exerted a remarkable influence on English criticism from the time of Dryden onwards.

us feel that genius is indeed something more than earthly:

> *And as imagination bodies forth*
> *The forms of things unknown, the poet's pen*
> *Turns them to shapes and gives to airy nothing*
> *A local habitation and a name.*

In such a passage we seem to behold him standing up, a figure of colossal stature, gazing at us over the heads of the intervening generations. He transcends the flight of time and the laborious building up of meanings, and, picking up a part of the outlook of an age which is to succeed his by nearly two hundred years, gives it momentary expression before he lets it drop again. That mystical conception which the word embodies in these lines—a conception which would make imagination the interpreter and part creator of a whole unseen world—is not found again until the Romantic Movement has begun.

And then it had to be reached slowly. Seventy years after Shakespeare wrote we find the philosopher, Henry More, cautiously distinguishing from other kinds of imagination 'that Imagination which is most free, such as we use in Romantick Inventions'. 'Imagining', wrote Dryden, 'is in itself the very height and life of poetry'; and in 1712 Addison published in the *Spectator* his papers on 'The Pleasures of the Imagination', in which he used the two words *fancy* and *imagination* synonymously, describing in one of the essays how, because of the faculty of which they are the names,

'. . . our Souls are at present delightfully lost and bewildered in a pleasing Delusion, and we walk about like the inchanted Hero of a Romance, who sees beautiful Castles, Woods, and Meadows; and at the same time hears the warbling of Birds, and the purling of Streams; but upon the finishing of some secret Spell, the fantastic Scene breaks up, and the disconsolate Knight finds himself on a barren Heath, or in a solitary Desart.

The tendency among critics to use this sort of imagery, or words suggestive of it, when writing of the *fancy* and the *imagination*, rapidly increased. Dryden had already distinguished the 'fairy' way of writing, and from Addison's time we constantly hear writers and their art referred to in terms of *fairyland, enchantments, magic, spells, wands, ...* Shakespeare, we are told by one writer, is 'a more powerful magician than his own Prospero'. 'The world is worn out to us,' wrote Young. 'Where are its formerly sweet delusions, its airy castles, and glittering spires?' And five years later he assured us that 'the pen of an original writer, like Armida's wand, out of a barren waste calls a blooming spring'.

But as the Romantic impulse grew older and crystallized into a philosophy—when the child which had germinated, as feeling, among the ignorant many who spoke the Romance languages, after passing through its Elizabethan adolescence, achieved self-conscious maturity, as thought, among the learned few who were familiar with the complicated literary languages of modern Europe—the need was felt for some way of distinguishing what were merely 'sweet delusions' from the more perdurable productions of the Romantic spirit. And this Coleridge achieved by his famous distinction between *fancy* and *imagination*. *Fancy,* since his day, has meant rather the power of inventing illustrative imagery—the playful adornment, as it were, of Nature; but *imagination* is the power of creating from within forms which themselves become a part of Nature—'Forms', as Shelley put it,

> *more real than living man,*
> *Nurslings of immortality.*

The next step in the meaning of this word was really taken on the day upon which Coleridge, with his head full of ancient witchery, was introduced to another poet with his heart full of mountains. Under their joint influence we can behold that despised habit of looking at life through the spectacles of the old Romances, the mysterious faculty of superimposing on Nature a magical colour or mood created in the observer by the *fictions* of genius or the myths of bygone ages, expanding until it includes the contemplation of Nature impassioned by any effluence arising from within—it may be emotion or it may be the individual memory. It was the philosophy of the Lake School that the perception of Nature—that is to say of all in Nature that is not purely mechanical—depends upon what is brought to it by the observer. Deep must call unto deep. To a creation apprehended as automatic by the senses and the reason, only *imagination* could

> *Add the gleam,*
> *The light that never was on sea or land;*

for imagination was 'essentially vital, even as all objects (*as* objects) are essentially fixed and dead'.[1]

[1] Coleridge: *Biographia Literaria.*

Imagination was, in fact, *organic*; and the application of this adjective to the inner world has not been traced farther back than Coleridge, who, in his lectures on Shakespeare's plays, emphasized the mistake of confounding 'mechanical regularity with organic form'. But perhaps the most brilliant, even epigrammatic, expression which has ever been given to the everlasting war between the unconscious, because creative, vital principle and the conscious, because destructive, calculating principle, is contained in four lines from a little poem of Wordsworth's called *The Tables Turned*:

> *Sweet is the lore which nature brings:*
> *Our meddling intellect*
> *Mis-shapes the beauteous forms of things—*
> *We murder to dissect.*

And so it is in the philosophy and poetry of Romanticism that we first feel a true understanding, not indeed of the process itself, but of the results of that process, which has been traced in this book under the name of 'internalization'. Slowly the divers of the Romantic expedition brought up to the surface of consciousness that vast new cosmos which had so long been blindly forming in the depths. It was a cosmos in which the spirit and spontaneity of life had moved out of Nature and into man. The magic of Persia, the Muses of Greece, the witches and fairies and charms and enchantments of Romance—all these had been locked safely in man's bosom, there to sleep until the trump of Romanticism sounded its call to imagination to give back their teeming life to Nature. 'O Lady', wrote Coleridge in that most heartrending of all poems, wherein, like the disconsolate knight awaking on the barren heath, he reports the decay in himself of this very power:

> *O Lady! we receive but what we give,*
> *And in our life alone does nature live:*
> *Ours is her wedding-garment, ours her shroud!*
>   *And would we aught behold, of higher worth,*
> *Than that inanimate cold world allowed*
> *To the poor loveless, ever-anxious crowd,*
>   *Ah! from the soul itself must issue forth*
> *A light, a glory, a fair luminous cloud*
>   *Enveloping the Earth—*
> *And from the soul itself must there be sent*
>   *A sweet and potent voice, of its own birth,*
> *Of all sweet sounds the life and element.*

And this re-animation of Nature was possible because the imagination was felt as *creative* in the full religious sense of the word. It had itself assisted in creating the natural forms which the senses were now contemplating. It had moved upon the face of the waters. For it was 'the repetition in the finite mind of the eternal act of creation'—the Word made human.

In tracing the semantic history of important words like these, we must not forget that nine-tenths of the words comprising the vocabulary of a civilized nation are never used by more than at most one-tenth of the population; while of the remaining tithe nine-tenths of those who use them are commonly aware of about one-tenth of their meanings. Nevertheless it is just by following those meanings to the high-water mark which they have reached in a few eager minds that we can observe what may fairly be called changes in the general consciousness. It is true that the new meanings must filter through a graduated hierarchy of imaginative literature, literary journalism, reviews, sermons, journalism, popular novels, advertisements, radio, and cinema captions before what is left of them reaches the general public; but the amount that *is* left, and the spell which is accordingly exerted on the many, depends on how far they have first been carried by the few. A hundred and fifty or more years ago, when mountains were still 'horrid', the foundations of the present economic structure of Switzerland were being quietly laid by the dreams of a few Lake poets and their brother Romantics. And incidentally the extraordinary load of meaning often borne by the word *dream* itself, in phrases like *dreamland, my dreams, the land of my dreams,* . . . is no doubt traceable ultimately to the use of this word by the great Romantics. When Shelley wrote:

> *Through the cold mass*
> *Of marble and of colour his[1] dreams pass . . .*

and

> *He hath awakened from the dream of life . . .*

he was also, we might say, writing the greater part of a good many twentieth-century drawing-room ballads.

Others today are fascinated by their *dreams*, because they regard them as messengers from that mysterious inner world in which, like the Christians of old, they are beginning to divine depths hitherto unimagined. They feel 'forces' at work there which they are tempted to personify in terms of ancient myth—*Ahriman, Lucifer, Oedipus, Psyche,*

[1] I.e. man's; the allusion is, of course, to plastic and visual art.

and the like. But outside the significant adjective *sub-conscious*, which has almost certainly come to stay, the effect which such tendencies may have on the English language remains a tale to be told a hundred years hence. The numerous secondary implications unfolding within *dream*, however, its popularity, and its obvious power of suggesting images, must interest us as further symptoms of a now almost universal consciousness of at any rate the existence of such an 'inner' world. In some lines written as a preface to the *Recluse*—the long, unfinished philosophical poem of which the *Prelude* and the *Excursion* were to form parts—Wordsworth has described the holy awe which he, for one, entertained as he realized that he must now set out to explore this world:

> Urania, I shall need
> Thy guidance, or a greater Muse, if such
> Descend to earth or dwell in highest heaven!
> For I must tread on shadowy ground, must sink
> Deep—and, aloft ascending, breathe in worlds
> To which the heaven of heavens is but a veil.
> All strength—all terror, single or in bands,
> That ever was put forth in personal form—
> Jehovah—with his thunder, and the choir
> Of shouting Angels, and the empyreal thrones,
> I pass them unalarmed. Not Chaos, not
> The darkest pit of lowest Erebus,
> Nor aught of blinder vacancy, scooped out
> By help of dreams—can breed such fear and awe
> As fall upon us often when we look
> Into our Minds, into the Mind of Man—
> My haunt, and the main region of my song.

AFTERWORD

So many books on words have appeared since the first edition of *History in English Words* that it would be a mistake to attempt a bibliography. The following remarks introduced the brief, selective and inadequate bibliography which was appended to the first edition.

'The immense debt which the foregoing pages owe to the *Oxford English Dictionary*—now practically complete—is, I hope, too obvious from the text to need further emphasis. Without access to that unrivalled monument of imaginative scholarship a great deal of the first part, and nearly all the second part, of this book could never have been even attempted. Readers who wish to study history in English words for themselves should lose no opportunity of consulting its fascinating volumes. And in case the fear of wearisome repetition has induced me to mislead, I should like to take advantage of this opening to point out that the *O.E.D.* is the authority for practically all the English etymological and semantic material on which my book is based. For example, the incautious but conveniently brief statement that such a word "was first used by" Chaucer or "first appeared in" the fourteenth century must be regarded as the abbreviated form of a longer statement to the effect that the earliest illustrative quotation given in the *O.E.D.* under the heading of the word in question is drawn from Chaucer or from a book written during that century.

'On the subject as a whole—history, and the outlook of men upon the world, as they are embodied in the histories of words—comparatively few people seem to have written in English. Trench led the way with his little book *On the Study of Words*, which is interesting, both for itself and because the Archbishop was the first to attach as much or more importance to the semantic than to the etymological side of his subject, being, in fact, himself the originator of the *Oxford Dictionary*. Max Müller's numerous essays and writings are fresh and keen and full of interest. The material adduced by both these writers should always be verified by reference to the *Dictionary*.

'I do not know if anyone has hitherto attempted to treat the subject chronologically and systematically, apart from one solitary English writer, Mr. Pearsall Smith. To his invaluable little book, *The English Language* (Home University Library), I am indebted throughout, not only for very much of my material, but also for many extremely fruitful suggestions as to the best way of dealing with it. I have also made extensive use of two essays ('English Words Abroad' and 'Four Romantic Words'), printed in *Words and Idioms* (Constable), of which, as of *The English Language*, it would, in my opinion, be very difficult to speak too highly, partly because of the imaginative treatment of the material and partly because of its solid background of careful scholarship and wide reading. It is a great pleasure to acknowledge here the more direct and personal help which I have been fortunate enough to receive from time to time from this distinguished writer.

Afterword

'For the rest, I have attempted to skim over such a wide area that a full bibliography is impossible. As an introduction to a closer study of the English language, the late Henry Bradley's *The Making of English* is practically indispensable. Skeat's *Etymological Dictionary* and *Concise Etymological Dictionary* (of which it is important to get the latest editions), and Weekly's *Etymological Dictionary of Modern English* are extremely useful works of reference, while for those who wish to acquire some sort of *feeling* for the relationship between apparently dissimilar Aryan words, such as *wheel* and 'kuklos', *brother* and 'frater', Skeat's *Primer of Classical and English Philology* (Clarendon Press) is inexpensive, brief, and to the point. . . .'

'It remains to add that such efficiency and precision as this little volume may possess have been increased by the kindness of my wife, who assisted me in the irksome task of indexing it, and of my father, who undertook the equally exacting business of reading the sheets.'

INDEX

Words printed in *italics* in the Index will be found italicized in the text also, unless the page number is between brackets. This signifies that on the page in question the word is used or referred to *incidentally*, and may or may not be typographically distinguished.

225

Index

229

Index

232

234

Index

236

239